In **Tibetan Sage**, T. Lobsang Rampa recollects his experiences as a young boy, when he travelled with his guide, the Lama Mingyar Dondup, into a timeless world hidden in caves at the peak of a Tibetan mountain.

The young boy witnesses visions and phenomena of the past and future. The weird and wonderful gadgets found in the caves prompt a series of long speeches from the Lama, on subjects as diverse as transmigration; the languages of Atlantis; the evils of petroleum; modern chocolate machines; the wise men of Tibet; television; space travel; and the two World Wars.

Lobsang Rampa and the Lama finally leave the caves and descend the mountain. Tibetan Sage, like his other works, reveals much of the mind and personality of Lobsang Rampa.

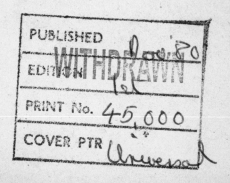

Also by T. Lobsang Rampa

Tibetan Sage

T. Lobsang Rampa

CORGI BOOKS

A DIVISION OF TRANSWORLD PUBLISHERS LTD

TIBETAN SAGE

A CORGI BOOK   0   552   11563   0

First publication in Great Britain

PRINTING HISTORY
Corgi edition published 1980

Copyright © T. Lobsang Rampa

This book is set in Century 10 on 11 pt.

Corgi Books are published by Transworld Publishers Ltd., Century
House, 61–63 Uxbridge Road, Ealing, London, W5 5SA

Made and printed in Canada by Universal Printers Ltd., Winnipeg.

Dedicated to
My Very Good Friend
Gertrud Heals

FOREWORD

People hooted and jeered when, some few years ago, I wrote in *The Third Eye* that I had flown in kites. One would have thought that I had committed a great crime in saying that. But now—well, we look about and we can see people flying in kites. Some of them are high above the water being towed by a speed boat. Yet others are kites with a man aboard, he stands on the edge of a cliff or high piece of ground, and then he jumps off and he is actually flying in a kite. Nobody says now that Lobsang Rampa was right, but they certainly did hoot when I wrote about kite flying.

There have been quite a number of things which were 'science fiction' a few years ago, but now—well, now they are almost everyday occurrences. We can have a satellite in space, and in London we can pick up the television programmes from the USA or from Japan. I predicted that.

We also now have had a man, or rather men, walking on the Moon. All my books are true, and they are gradually being proved true.

This book is not a novel. It is not science fiction. It is the absolutely unvarnished truth of what happened to me, and I again state that there is no author's licence in the book.

I say this book is true, but you may want to believe it to be science fiction or something like that. Well, fine, you are quite at liberty to have a good laugh and call it science fiction, and perhaps before you have actually finished reading the book some event will occur which will prove my books true. But I will tell you now that I will not answer any questions about this book. I have had such an enormous mail about the other books, and people do not even put in return postage and, with postal rates as they are at present, sometimes it takes more to reply to a reader's letter than he paid for the book in the first case.

Well, here is the book. I hope you like it. I hope you find it believable. If you do not find it believable it may be that you have not yet reached the necessary stage of evolution.

CHAPTER ONE

"Lobsang! LOBSANG!!" Dimly I seemed to swim up from the depths of a sleep of exhaustion. It had been a terrible day, but now—well, I was being called. Again the voice broke in, "Lobsang!" But I suddenly felt commotion about me, I opened my eyes and thought the mountain was falling on top of me. A hand reached out and a quick jerk lifted me from my place of rest and swung me rapidly aside, barely in time, too, because a massive rock with sharp edges slid down behind me and ripped off my robe. Quickly I stumbled to my feet and in a half-daze followed him to a little ledge at the far end of which was a very small hermitage.

About us rocks and snow came pelting down. Suddenly we saw the bent figure of the old hermit hurrying as fast as he could toward us. But no, a huge collection of rocks rolled down the mountain and swept away the hermitage and the hermit and the projecting rock on which the hermitage had stood. The rock was about two hundred feet in length, and it was swept away as a leaf is swept away in a gale.

My Guide, the Lama Mingyar Dondup, was holding me firmly by the shoulders. About us was darkness, not a glimmer of starlight, no gleam of a flickering candle from the houses of Lhasa. Everything was dark.

Suddenly there was a fresh barrage of immense rocks and sand, snow, and ice. The ledge upon which we so precariously stood tipped toward the mountain, and we felt ourselves sliding, sliding, we seemed to be

9

for ever sliding, and at last we came to a hearty bump. I think I blacked-out for a time because I suddenly came to my senses again thinking of the circumstances which had caused us to go to this very remote hermitage.

We had been at the Potala playing with a telescope which had been given to the Dalai Lama as a goodwill present from an English gentleman. Suddenly I saw prayer flags waving high up on the mountain side, they seemed to be waving in some sort of a code. Quickly I passed the telescope to my Guide and pointed up to the waving flags.

He stood there with the telescope braced against the wall of the topmost level of the Potala. He stood there for some time staring, and then he said, "The hermit is in need of help, he is ill. Let us inform the Abbot and say that we are ready to go." Abruptly he closed the telescope and gave it to me to put back in the Dalai Lama's storeroom of special gifts.

I ran with the thing, being particularly careful not to trip and not to drop that telescope, the first I had ever seen. And then I went out and filled my pouch with barley, checked that my tinder were adequate, and then I just hung around waiting for the Lama Mingyar Dondup.

Soon he appeared with two bundles, one great heavy bundle which he had on his shoulders and a smaller bundle which he put on my shoulders. "We will go by horse to the foot of that mountain, and then we shall have to send the horses home and climb—climb. It will be quite a hard climb, too, I have done it before." We got on our horses, and rode down the steps to where the Outer Ring of roads surrounds Lhasa. Soon we reached the turning off point and, as I always did, I took a quick look toward the left to the home where I had been born. But there was no time to think about it now, we were on a mission of mercy.

The horses began to labour, to pant and to snort. The climbing was too much for them, their feet kept slipping on the rocks. At last, with a sigh, the Lama

Mingyar Dondup said, "Well, Lobsang, the horses finish here. From now on we depend upon our own weary feet." We got off the horses and the Lama patted them and told them to return home. They turned about and trotted back along the path with renewed life at the thought of going home instead of having to climb further.

We rearranged our bundles and checked over our heavy sticks, any crack or flaw which had developed could prove fatal so we checked them, and checked the other things we were carrying. We had our flint and our tinder, we had our food supply, and so at last without a backward look we started climbing, climbing up the hard, hard mountain rock. It seemed to be made of glass, it was so hard and so slippery. We put our fingers and our toes in any little crevice and gradually, barking our shins and scraping our hands, we made our way up to a ledge. Here we stopped for a time to regain our breath and our strength. A little stream came from a crevice in the rock so we had a drink, and then we made some tsampa. It was not very savoury, it had to be made with cold, cold water, there was no room on the ledge for fire-making. But with our tsampa and a drink we felt refreshed again and discussed which way we should climb. The surface was smooth, and it seemed impossible that anyone could ever climb up that face, but we set to as had others before us. Gradually we inched upwards, upwards, gradually the tiny speck which had been visible to us became larger and larger until we could see individual rocks which formed the hermitage.

The hermitage was perched on the very end of a rocky spur which stood out from the side of the mountain. We climbed up under it, and then with immense effort we reached the side of the spur where we sat for several moments gasping for breath because here we were high above the Plain of Lhasa and the air was rarified and bitterly cold. At last we felt able to stand again, and we made our way much more easily this time until we reached the entrance of the hermitage.

The old hermit came to the door. I peered inside and I was absolutely amazed by the smallness of the room. Actually, there would not be room for three people so I resigned myself to staying outside. The Lama Mingyar Dondup nodded his approval, and I turned away as the door closed behind him.

Nature has to be attended to at all times, and sometimes Nature can be very pressing indeed, so I wandered around looking for "sanitary facilities". And, yes, right on the edge of that jutting rock there was a flat rock projecting even further out. It had a convenient hole in it which I could see had been manmade or man-enlarged. As I crouched down over that hole I could find a solution to something that had been puzzling me; on our way up we had passed a peculiar looking heap and what seemed to be yellowish shards of ice, some of them looked like yellowish ice rods. Now I was aware that those very puzzling mounds were evidence that men had lived in the hermitage for some time, and I gleefully added my own contribution.

That taken care of I wandered around and found the rock to be excessively slippery. But I walked along the path and came to what was obviously a moving rock. It was in the form of a ledge, and I wondered without any real interest why there should be a ledge of rock in that particular position. Being inquisitive I examined the rock with more than usual care, and I found my interest mounting because clearly it was manmade, and yet how could it be manmade? It was in such a strange position. So I just gave a desultory kick to the rock forgetting that I was bare-footed, so I nursed my injured toes for a few moments and then turned away from the ledge to examine the opposite side, the side up which we had climbed.

It was absolutely amazing and almost unbelievable to think that we had climbed up that sheer face. It looked like a sheet of polished rock as I gazed down, and I felt definitely queasy at the thought of climbing down.

I reached down to feel for my tinder box and flint,

12

and jerked to full awareness of my immediate situation. Here I was somewhere inside a mountain without a stitch of clothing, without the vital barley and bowl and tinder and flint. I must have muttered some un-Buddhistlike exclamation because I heard a whisper, "Lobsang, Lobsang, are you all right?"

Ah! My Guide, the Lama Mingyar Dondup was with me. Immediately I felt reassured, and replied, "Yes, I am here, I think I was knocked out when I fell, and I have lost my robe and all my possessions, and I haven't got the vaguest idea where we are or how we are going to get out. We need some light to see what can be done about your legs."

He said, "I know this passage very well indeed. The old hermit was the keeper of great secrets of the past and of the future. Here is the history of the world from the time it started until the time it ends." He rested for a few moments and then said, "If you feel along the left hand wall you will come to a ridge. Now if you push hard against that ridge it will slide back and give access to a big recess which has spare robes and ample barley. The first thing for you to do is to open the closet and feel for tinder and flint and candles. You will find them on the third shelf from the bottom. If we have light we can know how we can help each other." I carefully gazed along the left side of the Lama and then I touched the left hand wall of the passageway. It seemed to be a fruitless search, the wall was as smooth as could be, as smooth as if it had been made by human hands.

Just as I was about to give up I felt a sharp piece of rock. Actually I thumped my knuckles against it and it knocked off a piece of skin, but I pushed and pushed until I thought I would be unable to find the goods in the closet. With an extra special effort, and the rock slid sideways with a terrifying screech. Yes, there was a closet all right, and I could feel the shelves. First I concentrated on the third shelf from the bottom. Here there were butter lamps, and I located the flint and the tinder. The tinder was the driest stuff I had ever used and immediately it flared into flame. I lit the wick of a candle before very quickly extinguishing the tinder which was already reaching to burn my fingers.

"Two candles, Lobsang, one for you and one for me. There is an ample supply there, enough, if necessary, to last us a week." The Lama lapsed into silence, and I looked around to see what there was in the closet that we could use, and I saw a stave made of metal, iron it seemed to be, and I found I could hardly lift it. But it seemed to me that with a stave like that we might prise the rock off his legs, so I walked back with a candle and told the Lama what I was going to do. Then I went back for that metal bar. It seemed to me that it was the only means of freeing my Guide and friend from the grip of that boulder.

When I reached the boulder I put down the metal bar and went on hands and knees trying to find how I could obtain leverage. There were plenty of rocks about, but I doubted my own strength, I could hardly lift that bar as it was, but eventually I worked out a scheme; if I gave the Lama one of the staves he could perhaps push a rock under the boulder if I could elevate the thing a bit. He agreed with me that it might be possible, and he said, "It is the only thing we can do, Lobsang, because if I can't get free of this boulder here my bones will stay, so let's get busy with it now."

I found a fairly square piece of rock, it was about four hands in thickness. I put it right down against the boulder and then gave a wooden stave to the Lama for him to try with his part of the proceedings. We decided that, yes, if I could lift the boulder the victim should be able to push the square rock in under and that would give us enough room to get his legs out.

I pored over the boulder where it rested on the ground to see if there was any place where I could safely insert the bar. At last I found such a place, and I rammed the claw end in as far as I could under the boulder. It was a simple matter then to hunt around and find another boulder which I could put under the bar near the claw end.

"Ready," I yelled nearly stunning myself with the

echoes which came back, and I bore down with all my strength, with all my weight on the iron bar. No, it did not move, I was not strong enough, so I rested a moment or two and then I looked around for the heaviest rock that I could lift. Having found it I lifted it and carried it to the iron bar. There I balanced it on the extreme end of the bar and put all my weight on top of it, at the same time holding it from falling off the bar. To my delight there was a little hesitation and a little jerk, and slowly the bar moved down to ground level. The Lama Mingyar Dondup called out, "It's all right, Lobsang, I've got the block underneath and you can release the bar now, we can get my legs out."

I was overjoyed, and moved back to the other side of the boulder, and yes, it was off the Lama's legs, but the legs were raw and bleeding, and we feared that they were broken. Very, very gingerly we tried to move his legs, and he could move them so I got down and crawled under the boulder until I reached his feet. Then I suggested that he should lift himself up with his elbows and try to move backwards while I pushed on the soles of his feet. Gingerly, very gingerly, I pushed on the bottoms of his feet and it was obvious that, while the skin and flesh lacerations were severe, there were no broken bones.

The Lama kept trying to pull himself out from under the boulder. It was very difficult, and I had to push with all my strength against his feet and twist his legs a bit to avoid an outcrop of stone under the boulder. The outcrop, I surmised, was the only thing that had saved his legs from being absolutely squashed, and it was still giving us trouble. But at last, with more than a sigh of relief, his legs were quite clear and I crawled under the boulder to help him to sit on a ledge of rock.

Two little candles were not much to go by so I went back to that stone closet and got half a dozen more with a sort of basket in which to carry the things.

We lit all the candles and examined the legs very carefully; they were literally in shreds. From the thighs to the knees they were badly abraded, from the knees

15

to the feet the flesh was flapping because it had been cut into strips.

The Lama told me to go back and get some rags which were in a box, and he told me also to bring a jar with some paste in it. He described it exactly, and I went back to get the jar, the rags, and a few other things. The Lama Mingyar Dondup brightened up considerably when he saw that I had brought disinfecting lotion as well. I washed his legs from the hips down, and then at his suggestion I pushed the flapping strips of flesh back into place covering the bones—the leg bones had been showing very, very clearly, so I covered them with the flesh and then "glued" the flesh in position with the ointment stuff which I had brought. After about half an hour the ointment was almost dry and it looked as if the legs were in firm casts.

I tore some of the rags into strips and wound them around his legs to help keep the "plaster" in place. Then I took all the things back to the stone closet with the exception of our candles, eight in all. We blew out six and carried the others inside our robes.

I picked up our two wooden staves and gave them to the Lama who accepted them gratefully. Then I said, "I will move around to the other side of the boulder and then I shall be able to see how we are going to manage to get you out."

The Lama smiled and said, "I know all about this place, Lobsang, it has been here about a million years, and it was made by the people who first populated this country of ours. Provided no rocks have shifted and blocked the way we shall be safe enough for a week or two."

He nodded toward the direction of the outside world and said, "I think it is unlikely that we shall be able to get out that way, and if we cannot get out through one of the volcanic vents then some later explorers, in a thousand years or so, may find two interesting skeletons upon which to ponder."

I moved forward passing the tremendous side of the tunnel and the side of the boulder, and it was such a tight fit that I wondered how the Lama was going to get through. Still, I thought, where there is a will there is a way, and I came to the conclusion that if I crouched at the bottom of the boulder the Lama could walk over me and he would be that much higher up and so his legs and hips would get past the biggest bulge in the boulder. When I suggested it he was very, very reluctant, saying he was far too heavy for me, but after a few painful tries he came to the conclusion that there was just not any other way. So I piled a few small rocks around about the boulder so that I would have a fairly flat bed on which to crouch, and then, when I got down on my hands and knees, I told the Lama that I was ready. Very quickly he put one foot on my right hip and the other foot on my left shoulder, and with a quick movement he was through—past the boulder and on to clear ground the other side. I stood up and I saw that he was perspiring terribly with the pain and the fear that he might harm me.

We sat down for a few moments to regain our breath and our strength. We couldn't have any tsampa as our bowls had been lost, and so had our barley, but I remembered seeing such things in the stone closet. Once more I made a trip to the wall and raked through the wooden bowls that were there, picking the best one for the Lama and the next best one for myself. Then I gave them both a good scouring with fine sand which was so plentiful in that tunnel.

The two bowls I put on a shelf side by side, and then I put in a quite adequate amount of barley from the store kept in the closet. After that there was merely the task of lighting a small fire—there was flint and tinder in the closet, and firewood too—and then, with a hunk of butter which was in the closet, we mixed up the gooey mess which we called tsampa. Without a word we sat down and ate that little meal. Soon after we both felt much better and able to continue.

I checked our supplies, now replenished from that store closet, and, yes, we had a bowl each, tinder and flint, and a bag of barley each, and that really was all

17

we possessed in the world except for the two stout wooden staves.

Once again we set out, battered and bruised, and after what seemed walking for eternity we came to a stone right across the path, the end of the tunnel, or so I thought. But the Lama said, "No, no, this isn't the end, push on the bottom of that big slab and it will tilt from the middle, and then if we stoop we can get through." I pushed on the bottom as instructed, and with an awful screech the slab moved to a horizontal position and remained in that position. I held it for safety while the Lama painfully crawled under, and then I pushed the slab down again into its correct place.

Darkness, painful darkness which was made to appear even darker by the two little guttering candles. The Lama Mingyar Dondup said, "Put out your candle, Lobsang, and I will put out mine, and then we will see the daylight."

"See the daylight!" I thought that his experiences and the pain he must be suffering from had given him hallucinations, however I blew out my candle and for some time could smell the smoking wick which had been saturated with rancid butter.

The Lama said, "Now just wait a few moments and we shall have all the light we want." I stood there feeling an absolute fool, standing in what was now perfect darkness, not a glimmer of light from anywhere. I could have called it a "sounding darkness" because there seemed to be thump, thump, thump, squeeze, but that was dismissed from my mind as I saw what appeared to be a sunrise. Over at one side of what was apparently a room a glowing ball appeared. It was red and looked like red hot metal. Quickly the red faded into yellow and on to white, the white-blue of daylight. Soon everything was revealed in stark reality. I stood there with my mouth open marvelling at what I saw. The room, or whatever it was, occupied a greater space than did the Potala, the Potala could have been put into that room. The light was brilliant, and I was almost hypnotised by the decorations on the walls and by the strange things which littered the floor space without getting in one's way when one walked.

"An amazing place, eh, Lobsang? This was made more years ago than the mind of Man can comprehend. It used to be the headquarters of a special Race who could do space travel and just about everything else. Through millions of years it still works, everything is intact. Certain of us were known as the Guardians of the Inner Temple; this is the Inner Temple."

I walked over to examine the closest wall, and it appeared to be covered with writing of some sort, writing which I instinctively felt was not the writing of any race on Earth. The Lama picked up my thoughts by telepathy and replied, "Yes, this was built by the Race of Gardeners who brought humans and animals to this world."

He stopped speaking and pointed out a box set against a wall a little distance away. He said, "Will you go over there to that closet and fetch me two pieces of stick with a short piece across the top?" Obediently I walked across to the closet which he had pointed out. The door opened easily and I was absolutely fascinated by the contents. It seemed to be full of things for medical usage. In one corner there were a number of these sticks with the bars across one end. I picked out two, and saw that they would be able to support a man. I had no name such as crutches in those days, but I took two back to the Lama and he immediately put the short bars under his armpits, and about half way between the top and the bottom there was a sort of rod sticking out. The Lama Mingyar Dondup grasped these rods and said, "There you are, Lobsang, these things help the cripples to walk. Now I am going across to that closet and I can put proper casts on my legs, and then I shall be able to get about as usual while the flesh heals and while the bruises depart from the bones."

He walked over, and being naturally inquisitive I walked beside him. He said, "Fetch our staves and we will put them in this corner so that we can have them when we need them." He turned away from me and continued his poking about in the closet. I turned away, too, and went and picked up our staves and took them back to rest against the corner of that closet.

"Lobsang, Lobsang, do you think you could drag in our bundles and that steel bar? It is not iron, as you think, but something very much harder and stronger, and it is called steel." I turned once again and went to that slab through which we had entered. I pushed against the top of the thing and it swung to remain horizontal and motionless. It was no trouble for me to duck under the stone which I left in its horizontal position. The light was a blessing, it was a very real blessing because it shone quite a way down that tunnel and I could see my way past the side of the tunnel and the big boulder which had caused us so much trouble. Our bundles with all our possessions were on the opposite side, so with difficulty I got past the boulder and reached for the pouches. They seemed to be shockingly heavy, and I put it down to our weakened state through lack of food. First I took the two pouches back and left them just inside the doorway, and then I went back for the steel bar. I could hardly lift the thing, it made me pant and grunt like an old man, so I let one end drop while I held firmly to the other, and I found that by walking backwards and pulling on the steel bar with both hands I could just manage to make it move. It took me quite a time to get it around the boulder, but after that it was fairly easy going.

Now I had to push the bundles under the slab and into that immense room, and then I got the steel bar and decided I had never moved such a heavy weight in my life before. I manoeuvred it into the room and then pushed down the slab of door so that once again we had a smooth wall without an opening.

The Lama Mingyar Dondup had not wasted his time. Now his legs were encased in shiny metal, and once again he looked perfectly fit. "Lobsang, let us have a meal before we look round because we shall be here about a week. While you were fetching these things," he pointed to the bundles and the steel rod, "I have been in telepathic communication with a friend at the Potala, and he tells me a terrific gale is raging. He advised me to stay where we are until the gale has abated. The weather prophets said the storm would rage for about a week." I felt really gloomy about it because I was sick of this tunnel and not even the room could interest me much. In spite of the size of the room I was feeling a certain amount of claustrophobia which sounds impossible but was not. I felt like an animal in a cage. However, the pangs of hunger were stronger than any fears, and I watched with pleasure as the Lama made our meal. He made it better than anyone, I thought, and it was so nice to sit down to a hot meal. I took a mouthful of the stuff, which really is a polite name for tsampa, and marvelled at the flavour of it. It was a very pleasant flavour indeed, and I felt my strength coming back and my gloom disappearing. After I finished my bowlful the Lama said, "Have you had enough, Lobsang? You can have as much as you wish, there is plenty of food here, enough, in fact, to feed a small lamasery. I'll tell you about it sometime, but now—would you like some more?"

"Oh, thank you!" I replied. "I certainly could do with a little more, and that has such a pleasant taste to it. I have never tasted anything like that before."

The Lama chuckled as he turned away to get me more food, and then he actually burst out into a laugh. "Look, Lobsang," he said, "look at this bottle. It is best brandy kept entirely for medical purposes. I think that we can consider our incarceration here as warranting a little brandy to give flavour to the tsampa."

I took the bowl that he proffered to me and sniffed it appreciatively, but at the same time dubiously because I had always been taught that these intoxicating liquors were the works of the Devils, and now I was being encouraged to taste it. Never mind, I thought, its good stuff when one doesn't feel too fresh.

I set to and soon got in an awful mess. We had only our fingers, you know, nothing like a knife, fork or spoon, not even chopsticks, but fingers, and after meals

21

we used to wash our hands with fine sand which would take off tsampa with wonderful efficiency besides at times taking off a bit of skin if one was too energetic.

I scooped out tsampa, not with my fingers alone but I brought the palm of my right hand into play, and then suddenly—quite without warning—I fell over backwards. I like to say that I fell asleep through over-tiredness, but the Lama said I was dead drunk when he laughingly told the Abbot about it later. Drunk or not, I slept and slept and slept, and still when I awakened that wonderful golden light suffused the room. I gazed up at—well, I suppose it was the ceiling, but the ceiling was so far up I could not tell where it was. It was truly an immense room, as if the whole wretched mountain was hollow.

"Sunlight, Lobsang, sunlight, and it will work twenty-four hours a day. The light it gives is absolutely without heat, it is precisely the same temperature as the air around us. Don't you think it is better to have light like this than smelly, smoking candles?"

I looked about again and just could not see how there could be sunlight when we were entombed in a rock room, and I said as much. The Lama replied, "Yes, this is a marvel of marvels, I have known it all my life, but no one knows how it works. Cold light is a miraculous invention, and this was invented or discovered a million or so years ago. They developed a method of storing sunlight, and making it available even on the darkest nights. There is none of it in the city nor in the temple because we just do not know how to make it. This is the only place I know where there is this type of lighting."

"A million or so, you said. That is almost beyond my comprehension. I think it is a figure like a one or a two or a three, or something like that, followed by a number of noughts, six I think it is, but that's only a guess, and in any case it is so vast a number that I can't realise it. It doesn't count for anything for me. Ten years, twenty years, yes I can relate to that, but longer—no.

"How was this room made?" I asked as I trailed my

fingers idly over some inscription on the wall. I jumped back in fright as a certain click occurred and a part of the wall slid back.

"Lobsang! Lobsang! You have made a discovery. None of us who have been here knew there was another room attached to this." Cautiously we peered into the open doorway, and as soon as our heads passed the doorpost the light came on and I noted that as we left the first great room the light faded at our absence.

We looked about almost afraid to move because we did not know what perils there were or what traps we might fall into, but eventually we plucked up courage and walked over to a great "something" standing in the middle of the floor. It was a tremendous structure. Once it had been shiny, but now it had a dull grey glaze. It was about four or five men tall, and it looked something like two dishes, one on top of the other. We walked around and there at the far side we saw a grey metal ladder extending down from a doorway in the machine to the floor. I ran forward forgetting that as a young man in Holy Orders I should show more decorum, but I ran forward and hastily climbed the ladder without even bothering to see if it was safely fixed. It was. Once again as my head blocked the doorway lights came on inside the machine. The Lama Mingyar Dondup, not to be outdone, climbed up into the interior of the machine and said, "Ah, Lobsang, this is one of the Chariots of the Gods. You've seen them flitting about, haven't you?"

"Oh yes, sir," I replied. "I thought there were Gods traversing our Land to see that everything was all right, but, of course, I have never seen one as close as this before."

CHAPTER TWO

We looked about us and we seemed to be in a sort of corridor lined on both sides with lockers or closets, or something similar. Anyway, I pulled experimentally on a handle and a big drawer slid out as smoothly as if it had just been made. Inside there were all manner of strange devices. The Lama Mingyar Dondup was peering over my shoulder, he picked up one of the pieces and said, "Ah! This will be spare parts. I have no doubt that these lockers contain spare parts enough to make this thing work again." We pushed the drawer shut, and moved on. The light moved ahead of us and dimmed as we passed, and soon we came to a large room. As we entered it became brilliantly illuminated, and we both gasped, this was obviously the control room of the thing but what made us gasp was the fact that there were men about. One was sitting in what I imagined to be the control chair and he was peering at a meter on a board in front of him. There were quite a number of meters, and I surmised that he was just getting ready to take off. I said, "But how can these be millions of years old? These men look alive but soundly asleep."

There was another man sitting at a table and he had some large charts in front of him. He had his head held between his hands and his elbows rested on the table. We spoke in whispers. It was awesome, and our science was nothing but mumbo-jumbo compared to this.

The Lama Mingyar Dondup caught hold of one of the figures by the shoulder, and said, "I think these

24

men are in some form of suspended animation. I think they could be brought back to life, but I do not know how to do it, I do not know what would happen if I did know how to do it. As you know, Lobsang, there are other caves in this mountain range and we visited one with strange implements in it like ladders which, apparently, worked mechanically. But this beats anything I have seen so far, and as one of the senior Lamas who is responsible for maintaining these intact I can tell you that this one is the most wonderful of all, and I wonder if there are any other knobs that we should press to open other rooms. But let us have a good look in this one first. We have about a week, because I think it will take at least that long before I am fit to climb down the mountainside."

We went around looking at the other figures, seven of them in all, and they all gave the impression that they were ready to take off when something frightful occurred. It looked as if there had been an earthquake which toppled heavy rocks on what was probably a sliding roof.

The Lama stopped and approached another man who had a book—a notebook—in front of him. Obviously he had been writing the record of what was happening, but we could not read the writing, we had no basis for assuming that these things were letters, idiographs, or even just technical symbols. The Lama said, "In all our searches we have not found anything which would enable us to translate—wait a minute," he said with some unwonted excitement in his voice, "that thing over there, I wonder if that is a machine for speaking a record. Of course, I don't suppose that it will work after all these years, but we will try."

Together we moved over to the instrument which he had mentioned. We saw it was a form of box, and about half way down there was a line all the way around. Experimentally we pushed up on the surface above the line, and to our delight the box opened and inside there were wheels and one thing which seemed to be for the conveyance of a metal strip from one spool to another.

The Lama Mingyar Dondup peered down at the press-buttons arrayed along the front. Suddenly we nearly jumped out of our skins; we nearly turned and ran for it because a voice came from out of the top part of the box, a strange voice much, much different from ours. It sounded like some foreigner lecturing, but what he was lecturing about we did not know. And then—surprise again—noises came out of the box, music I suppose they would call it, but to us it sounded all discords. So my Guide pressed another button and the noise stopped.

We were both rather exhausted with what we had discovered and by an excess of excitement, so we sat down on what were obviously chairs and I felt panic because I seemed to sink right down in the chair as if I was actually sitting on air. As soon as we recovered from that shock the Lama Mingyar Dondup said, "Perhaps we should have some tsampa to cheer us up because I think both of us are exhausted." He looked about to see where we could light a little fire to warm up the tsampa, and he was soon rewarded because there was a cubicle off the control room and as he entered it the light came on. The Lama said, "I think this must have been where they prepared their food because all these buttons are not there for ornament, they are there for some useful purpose." He pointed to one button which had a picture of a hand held in the Stop position. Another button had a picture of flame, so he pushed the one with flame marked on it, and above that instrument there were various metal vessels. We took one down.

By this time we were feeling heat, and the Lama moved a hand about and finally said, "There you are, Lobsang, feel that, there is the heat for our cooking." I put my hand where he said, but a bit too close, and I jumped back in some alarm. But my Guide just laughed and put near-frozen tsampa in the metal container and then rested it on some bars over the hot thing underneath them. He added water, and soon we saw a little dribble of steam coming up from the dish. With that he pressed the button marked with the hand symbol, and immediately the red glow ceased. He took the metal dish off the heat source, and with a metal thing with a big dished end he ladled tsampa into our bowls. For some time there was no sound other than the noise we made eating.

With the tsampa finished I said, "I wish I could get a good drink, I am as thirsty as can possibly be."

By the side of the box which made heat we saw what seemed to be a big basin, and above there were two metal handles. I tried one and turned it in the only way it would go, and water, cold water, gushed out into the basin. I hastily turned the handle back and tried the other one which was of a reddish colour. I turned that and really hot water came out, so much so that I scalded myself, not very seriously, but I still scalded myself enough to make me jump, so I turned that handle back to its original position. "Master," I said, "if this is water it must have been here one of those millions of years that you talked about. How is it that we are able to drink it, it should be all evaporated or gone sour by now, but I find it quite pleasant."

The Lama replied, "Well, water can be kept good for years, how about the lakes and the rivers? They were water far beyond history, and I suppose this water is from an airtight container which means that it should stay palatable. I surmise that this ship had just come here for supplies, and perhaps for some repairs, because with the pressure of water that came out there must be quite a large amount in some storage tank. Anyway, we've got enough here to keep people busy for a month."

I said, "Well, if the water kept fresh there must be food here, perhaps that has kept fresh as well." I got up from the chair with some difficulty because it seemed to want to cling to me, but then I put my hands on the side of the chair—on the top of the armrests—and immediately I was not only released from the chair but I was shot up to a standing position. Having recovered from that marvel and shock, I went along feeling the walls in the little kitchen. I saw a lot of indentations which seemed to have no purpose. I put my finger in one and pulled, and nothing happened. I tried to pull it sideways, but no, the thing did not work, so I went to another one and I pushed my finger straight into the indentation and a panel slid aside. Inside that closet, or cabinet, or whatever the thing was called, there were a number of jars which seemed to be without any joins anywhere. There were transparent panels so that one could see what was inside. Obviously it was some sort of food, but how could food be preserved for a million years or more?

I puzzled and puzzled over the problem. There were pictures of foods that I had never seen or heard of, and some of the things were encased in a transparent container yet there seemed to be no way of opening the container. I went from one of these closets, cupboards, or storage rooms to another, and each time there was a fresh surprise. I knew what tea leaves were like, but here in one of the cabinets there were containers which I could see through the transparent sides contained tea leaves.

There were other surprises because some of these transparent containers had what was obviously cuts of meat inside them. I had never tasted meat and I longed to have a go at it to see, or rather to taste, what it was like.

I quickly tired of playing in the kitchen and I went in search of the Lama Mingyar Dondup. He had a book in his hand and he was frowning and in a state of intense concentration.

"Oh, Master," I said, "I have found where they keep their food, they have it stored in boxes that one can see through, but there is no way of opening them." He looked at me blankly for a moment and then burst out with a laugh. "Oh yes, oh yes," he said, "the packaging of the present day materials is nothing like the packaging of a million years ago. I have tasted dinosaur meat and it was as fresh as if from a newly killed animal. I will come with you shortly and we will investigate."

I walked around that control room and then I sat down to think things over. If these men were a million years old why had they not crumbled into dust? It was clearly ridiculous to say that these men were a million years old when they were absolutely intact and appeared to be fully alive and just awaiting an awakening. I saw that hung on the shoulders of each one there was a sort of small satchel, so I removed one from one of the "sleeping bodies" and I opened it. Inside there were curious bits of wire twisted in coils, and there were other things made of glass, and the whole thing made no sense at all to me. There was a rack inside full of buttons, pressbuttons, and I pressed the first one I saw. I screamed with fear; the body from which I had taken that satchel suddenly jerked and crumbled into fine, fine dust, the dust of a million years or more.

The Lama Mingyar Dondup came over to where I stood petrified with fright. He looked at the satchel, and he looked at the pile of dust, and then he said, "There are quite a number of these caves, I have visited a few of them and we have learned never to press a button until you know what it does, until you have worked it out by theory. These men knew that they were going to be buried alive in some tremendous earthquake, so the doctor of the ship would have gone to each man and put a survival kit on his shoulder. The men would then go into a state of suspended animation so that they would know nothing whatever of what was happening to them or around them, they would be as near dead as anyone could be without actually dying. They would be receiving adequate nourishment to keep the body functioning on a minute scale. But when you touched this button, which I see is a red button, you would have discontinued the supply of life force to the man in suspended animation. Having no longer a life force supply his age would come upon him suddenly, and he would immediately turn into a pile of dust."

We went around to the other men and we decided that there was nothing we could do for them because, after all, we were shut in the mountain and the ship

29

was shut in the mountain, and if these people came awake would they be a danger to the world? Would they be a danger to the lamaseries? These men, of course, were possessed of knowledge which would make them appear as Gods to us, and we were afraid of being made into slaves again because we had a very strong racial memory that we had been slaves at some time.

The Lama Mingyar Dondup and I sat together on the floor not speaking but each buried in his own thoughts. What would happen if we pressed this button, and what would happen if we pressed that button, and what sort of supply of energy could it be that would keep men alive and well nourished for more than a million years? Involuntarily we both shuddered at the same time, and then we looked at each other and the Lama said, "You are a young man, Lobsang, and I am an old man. I have seen much and I wonder what you would do in a case like this. These men are alive, there is no doubt about that, but if we bring them back to full life what if they are savage, what if they kill us because we have let one of their number die? We have to think this over most seriously, we can't read the inscriptions;" he stopped there because I had jumped to my feet in some excitement. "Master, Master," I cried, "I have found a book which seems to be a sort of dictionary of different languages, I wonder if it would help us." Without waiting for a reply I jumped up and rushed into a room near the kitchen, and there was this book looking as if it had just been produced. I grabbed it with two hands because it was heavy, and then I dashed back to the Lama, my Guide, with it.

The Lama took the book and with ill-concealed suppressed excitement he opened the pages. For some time he sat there absolutely absorbed in the book. At last he became aware that I was jumping about in extreme agitation wondering what it was and why he did not tell me.

"Lobsang, Lobsang, I'm sorry, I apologise to you," said the Lama, "but this book is the Key to everything, and what a fascinating tale it is. I can read it, it is

30

written in what seems to be our honorific language. The average person, of course, could not read honorific Tibetan, but I can and this ship is about two million years old. It works on energy obtained from light—any light, the light of the stars, the light of the sun, and it picks up energy from those sources which have already used that energy and passed it on.

"These men," he referred again to the book, "were an evil lot, they were servants of the Gardeners of the World. But it is the old tale, men and women, men want women just as women want men, but this ship was crewed by men who had abandoned the great mothership and this, actually, is what they term a lifeboat. The food would be quite safe to eat, and the men could be awakened, but no matter how long they have been here they are still renegades because they tried to find women who would be much too small for them and their association with the women would be an absolute torture to the latter. They wonder if their life satchels will work or whether it will have been switched off automatically from the ship which they refer to as the mothership. I think we shall have to experiment a bit and read some more because it seems clear to me that if these men are allowed to live then they have such knowledge that they can do us harm which we could never overcome because these people treat us as cattle, as things on which to carry out genetic experiments. Already they have done harm because of their sexual experiments with our women, but you are too young to know all about that yet."

I wandered around the place. The Lama was lying down on the floor to ease his legs which were giving quite a bit of trouble. I wandered around, and eventually I came to a room which was all green. There was a very peculiar looking table there with a great big light over it, and there were what appeared to be glass boxes all over the place. "Hmm," I thought to myself, "this must be where they repair their sick people, I'd better go and tell the Boss about this." So I bustled off and told the Lama Mingyar Dondup that I had found a very peculiar room, a room that was all green and which had strange things encased in what looked like glass but wasn't. Slowly he got to his feet and with the help of the two staves made his way to the room I had discovered.

As soon as I entered—I was leading the way—lights came on, lights just like daylight, and the Lama Mingyar Dondup stood there in the doorway with a look of immense satisfaction on his face. "Well done, Lobsang, well done," he said, "that is two discoveries which you have made. I am sure this information will be well received by His Holiness, the Dalai Lama." He walked around looking at various things, picking up other things, and peering at the contents of some of the—well, I do not know what to call them—some of the things in glass cubes were absolutely beyond my comprehension. But at last he sat down on a low chair, and he became enthralled in a book which he had taken from a shelf. "How is it," I asked, "that you can understand a language which you say is at least a million years old?"

With an effort he put aside the book for a moment while he thought over my question. Then he said, "Well, it's quite a long tale, you know, Lobsang. It leads us back throughout the bylanes of history, it leads us through paths which even some of the Lamas cannot follow. But briefly it is like this: This world was ready to be colonised and so our Masters—I must call them Masters because they were the head men of the Gardeners of the Earth and of other worlds—dictated that a certain species should be grown on the Earth, and that certain species was us.

"In a far distant planet, right out of this Universe, preparations were made and a special ship was made which could travel at an absolutely unbelievable speed, and we, as human embryos, were packed in the ship. Somehow the Gardeners, as they were called, brought them to this world and then we do not know what happened between the time of the arrival of the embryos and the first creatures that could be called human.

"But during their absence from their home world much occurred. The old ruler, or "God", was aged and there were certain people of evil intent who wanted his power, and they managed to get rid of that God and put another one—their own puppet—to rule in his place. His ruling, of course, to be dictated by these renegades.

"The ship came back from the Earth and found things very different, they found they were not welcome and the new ruler wanted to kill them so they would be out of the way. But instead the Gardeners who had just returned from the Earth grabbed a few women of their own size and they took off again for the Earth Universe (there are many, many different universes, you know, Lobsang.)

"Arrived at the world where they had been growing humans they set up their own dominion, they built various artefacts like pyramids with which they could keep radio watch over anything coming in the direction of the Earth. They used the humans that they had grown as slaves, they did all the work and the Gardeners just sat back in luxury and told the human slaves what to do.

"The men and women, perhaps we should call them the supermen and the superwomen, got tired of their own partners, and there were many liasons which led to bickering and all manner of trouble. But then from outer space and undetected by the pyramid searchers a space ship appeared. It was a vast ship, and it settled down so that people could come out of it and start to build habitations. The people who were the first on the Earth resented the appearance of these other space men and women, and so, from a battle of words, there came a battle of people. The trouble went on for some time, and the most devilish inventions were made. At last the people in the big space ship could not put up with the trouble any longer so they sent out a number of space ships which apparently were stored ready for such an occasion, and they dropped terrible bombs wherever these other space people were living.

"The bombs were a very advanced form of atom

bomb, and within sight of where the bomb had exploded everything became dead. There was a purple glare coming from the land and the space men and women who had caused this got back in their giant space ship and left the area.

"For a hundred years or more there was hardly any form of life on the Earth in the bombed areas, but when the radiations' effects lessened these people crept out in fear and trembling wondering what they would see. They settled down to a form of farming using wooden ploughs and things like that."

"But Master," I said, "you say the world is more than fifty million years old; well, there are such a lot of things I do not understand at all, for instance these men—well, we don't know how old they are, we don't know how many days, weeks, or centuries they have been here, and how can food have been kept fresh all these years? Why didn't the men crumble to dust?"

The Lama laughed. "We are an illiterate people, Lobsang. There used to be very much more clever people on this Earth, there have been several civilisations, you know. For instance," he pointed to a book on the shelf, "this book tells about medical and surgical practises of a type we in Tibet have never even heard of, and we were one of the first people to be put on this Earth."

"Then why are we up so high, why is our life so hard? Some of those picture books you brought back from Katmandu show all sorts of things, but we have no knowledge of things like that, we have nothing on wheels in Tibet."

"No, there is an old, old saying that when Tibet permits wheels to be brought into the country then Tibet will be conquered by a very unfriendly race. Their predictions were just as if they could see into the future, and I am going to tell you, young man, that they could see into the future and they had instruments here which will show you what happened in the past, what is happening now, and what will happen in the future," my Guide said.

"But how can things last so long? If things are left,

well, they decay, they fall to pieces, they become useless through disuse like the Prayer Wheel in that old lamasery, that you showed me, a beautiful piece of work corroded and immovable. How could these people stop things from decaying, how could they provide the power to keep things working? Look at the way the lights come on as soon as we enter a room; we have nothing like that, we use stinking butter candles or rush lights, and yet here we have light which is as good as daylight, and it is not being generated anywhere because in that book you showed me there were pictures of machines that worked in a magnetic field and generated what you call electricity. We don't have that. Why is it that we are so isolated?" I was puzzled.

The Lama was silent for a moment, and then he said, "Yes, you will have to know all these things, you are going to be the most educated Lama that there ever was in Tibet, you are going to see the past, the present, and the future. In this particular range of the mountains there are a number of these caves and at one time they were all joined together by tunnels. It was possible to move from one cave to another and have light and fresh air the whole time, no matter where we were. But this land of Tibet was once down by the sea, people lived on flat land with just a very few low hills, and the people of that earlier Age had sources of power quite unknown to us. But there came a terrific catastrophe because beyond our land scientists of a country called Atlantis let off a tremendous explosive and that ruined this world."

"Ruined this world?" I said. "But our land is all right, how is it ruined, how is the world ruined?"

The Lama got up and went to a book. There were such a lot of books here, and he went to a book and found certain pictures. Then he said, "Look, this world once was covered with cloud. There was never a sight of the sun, we knew nothing about the stars. But then in those days people lived hundreds of years, not like now dying as soon as they have learned anything. People die off now because of the evil radiations from the sun, and because our protecting cloud cover had gone;

then dangerous rays came and saturated the world bringing all sorts of diseases, all sorts of mental aberrations. The world was in turmoil, the world writhed under the impact of that tremendous explosion. Atlantis, which was a long way from here on the other side of the world, Atlantis sank beneath the ocean, but we of Tibet—well, our land went up twenty-five to thirty thousand feet above sea level. People became less healthy and for a long time people fell dead because there was not enough oxygen at this height for them, and because we were nearer the skies and where we were the radiations were stronger." He stopped for a moment and rubbed his legs which were paining him a great deal, and then he said, "There is a far part of our land which stayed at sea level and the people there became more and more different from us, they became almost stupid in their mentality, they had no temples, they did not worship the Gods, and even now they go about in skin boats catching seals and fish and other forms of life. There are some immense creatures with enormous horns on their heads, and these people killed many of them and ate their flesh. When other races came along they called these far-northern people Eskimos. Our part of Tibet had the best people, priests, and wise men, and doctors of great renown, and the part which was sheared away from Tibet and sank to sea level, or rather, stayed at sea level, had the lesser mentalities, the ordinary workers, the ordinary people, the hewers of wood and the drawers of water. They have remained in almost the same state for more than a million years. They gradually crept out and set about making a living on the surface of the Earth. They set up small farms and within a hundred or so years things appeared to be normal and settled down.

"Before we go any further in our discussions I will ask you to look at my legs, they are paining me a great deal and I have a book here which shows wounds something like mine. I can read enough of it to be aware that I have an infection." I looked at him hard because what could I, an ordinary chela, do for such a great man? But there it was, I took the rag wrappings off his legs and recoiled at what I saw. The legs were covered in puss, and the flesh looked very, very angry indeed. In addition the legs below the knees were very swollen. The Lama said, "Now, you will have to follow my instructions exactly. First of all we have to get something which will disinfect these legs. Fortunately everything here is in good condition, and up on that shelf," he pointed, "you will find a jar with some writing on the glass. I think you will find it is the third container from the left on the second shelf down. Bring it over and I will see if it is the right one."

Obediently I went over to the shelves and slid back a door which appeared to be made of glass. Now, I didn't know much about glass because we had very, very little of it in Tibet. Our windows were either covered with oiled paper to make them translucent and so admit some light to the rooms, but most people had no windows because they could not afford the cost of bringing glass all the way across the mountains, glass which had to be purchased in India.

I slid the glass door aside, and then I looked at the bottles and—yes—this is the one, I thought, so I took it over to him. He looked at it and read some directions, then he said, "You'd better pass me that big container standing there on the side upside-down. Wash it out well first. There is unlimited water, remember, so you wash it out, and then put a little water in, about three bowlfuls of water." So I did that, I scoured the container thing which was already spotless, and I guessed three bowlfuls of water and took it back to him. He, to my profound amazement, did something to the bottle and the top came off! I exclaimed, "Oh! You've broken the thing, shall I try to find an empty one?"

"Lobsang, Lobsang," said the Lama, "you really do make me laugh. If there is something in this jar then there has to be a means of getting it in and then getting it out. This is merely what you call a stopper. I will use this stopper upside-down and then it becomes a measuring device. Do you see that?"

I looked at the stopper which he had upside-down, and yes, I could see it was a measuring thing of some kind because there were marks all the way down. So then he continued, "We shall have to have some cloth. Now in that cupboard, if you open it, you will find a lot of bundles. Open the cupboard door so that I can see."

This door was not made of glass and it was not made of wood, it seemed to be something between the two, but I pulled the door open and then I saw that there were a lot of bundles in orderly array. The Lama said, "Bring over that blue one, and to the right of it there is a white one, bring that as well." He looked at me, looked at my hands, and said, "And go to the tap and wash your hands. By the tap you will see a cake of white material. Wet your hands and then wet that cake and smear it over your hands, being very careful to get your nails clean."

I did all that, and I was quite interested in seeing how much lighter my skin appeared. It was something like seeing a negro for the first time all black, and then seeing the palms of his hands which were pink. Now my hands were just about pink, and I was just going to wipe them on my robe when the Lama said, "Stop!" He pointed to something that he had taken out of the white package. "Wipe your hands on that and don't you dare touch your filthy old robe after you have wiped your hands dry. You have to have clean hands for doing this job."

It was really interesting because he had a clean sheet of cloth-stuff on the floor, and he had various things on it, a basin, a thing like a scoop, and another thing which I did not understand at all; it is so hard to describe because I had never even seen such a thing, but it appeared to be a tube of glass with markings on it, and at one end there seemed to be a steel needle while at the other end there was a knob. In the tube, which was obviously hollow, there was some coloured liquid which bubbled and sparkled. The Lama said, "Now listen carefully to me; you will have to clean out

38

the flesh all the way down to the bone. Now here we have the fruits of the wonderful, wonderful, very advanced science, and we are going to make full use of it. Take this styrette and pull the end off the tube—wait, I will do it for you—and then you stick that needle in my leg just here," he indicated a particular spot, "and that will make the leg numb, otherwise I should probably faint from the excruciating pain which this is going to cause. Now go to it."

I lifted the thing he had called a styrette, and I looked at the Lama and I shuddered. "No, no, I can't do it, I am so afraid of hurting you."

"Lobsang, you are going to be a medical lama, sometimes you will have to hurt people to cure them. Now do as I say and stick that needle in right up to the hilt. I will tell you if the pain is too much."

I picked up the thing again, and I was afraid I was going to faint, but—well—orders were orders. I took hold of the thing not too far from where the needle joined the body, and I closed my eyes and jabbed quickly. There was not a sound from the Lama, so I opened my eyes and found that he was smiling! "Lobsang, you made a very fine job of that, I felt not a twinge. You are going to be a success as a medical lama." I looked at him suspiciously thinking that he was making fun of me, but I saw that, no, he was perfectly sincere in what he had said. He continued, "Now, we have given this long enough and this leg feels quite dead so it won't respond to pain. I want you to take those things, they are called forceps, by the way, and I want you to put a little of this liquid in a bowl and then wipe the leg thoroughly in a downward direction—downward, not up but down. You can press fairly hard and you will find that the pus comes away in lumps. Well, when you've got a nice pile of puss on the ground you'll have to help me move to a fresh spot."

I picked up the things he had called forceps and found that I could pick up a nice bundle of this cotton stuff. I carefully dipped it in the bowl and wiped his legs. It was incredible, absolutely incredible, how the pus and dried blood came pouring away from the leg, from the wounds.

I got that leg quite clean, the bone was clean and the flesh was clean. Then the Lama said, "This is a powder. I want you to shake the powder into the wounds so it gets as far as the bone. It will disinfect the legs and prevent more pus from forming. When you have done that you will have to bandage my legs with a bandage from that blue packet."

So we went on cleaning, cleaning, cleaning, shaking in this white dust, and then putting some plastic wrapping thing over the leg and after bandaging it, not too tightly but just tight enough. By the time I had finished I really was absolutely asweat, but the Lama was looking better.

After I had done one leg I did the other, and then the Lama said, "You'd better give me a stimulant, Lobsang. It's up on that top shelf and you just bring down one ampoule, an ampoule is a little container with a pointed end, and you snap off the pointed end and jab the ampoule against my flesh, anywhere."

So I did that and then I cleaned up all the pus and mess, and then I fell asleep on my feet.

CHAPTER THREE

My! The sun was hot indeed. "I shall have to find a shady spot," I muttered to myself. And then I sat up and opened my eyes and gazed about with blank astonishment. Where was I? What had happened? And then, as I saw the Lama Mingyar Dondup, it all came back to me, and I had thought perhaps it was just a dream. There was no sun, the place was lit by something which looked like sunlight coming through glass walls.

"You do look absolutely amazed, Lobsang," said the Lama. "I hope you have had a good rest." "Yes, Master," I replied, "but I am becoming more and more puzzled, and the more things are explained the more puzzled I become. For instance, this light coming from somewhere, it can't be stored up for a million years and then shine as brightly as the sun itself."

"There are a lot of things you will have to learn, Lobsang, you are a bit young yet but as we have arrived at this place—well, I will explain a bit to you. The Gardeners of the Earth wanted secret places so they could come to Earth unknown to the earthlings, and so when this was just a low heap of stone protruding above the ground they cut into the living stone by means of what will later be known as atomic torches. It melted out the rock and a lot of the grey surface outside is steam from the melted rock, and then when the cave was cut out to the right size it was allowed to cool, and it cooled with an absolutely glass-smooth surface.

"Having done the cavern which is big enough to take the Potala itself, they did some investigating and then they bored tunnels right along this rock range which in those days was almost covered by earth. It used to be possible to travel about two hundred and fifty miles through these tunnels, from cave to cave.

"Then there was this mighty explosion which rocked the Earth on its axis, and some places were drowned and other places rose up. We were fortunate in that the low hill became a mountain range. I have seen pictures of it and I will show them to you, but of course through the Earth movements some of the tunnels were forced out of alignment and one could no longer go the whole length as before. Instead we could visit perhaps two or three caves before emerging out on the mountain range and then walking a bit to where we knew the tunnel would continue. Time doesn't matter at all to us, as you know, so I am one of those who has been to about a hundred of these places and I have seen many, many strange things."

"But, Master," I said, "how can these things remain workable after a million or so years? No matter what we have, even a Prayer Wheel, deteriorates with time and use, and yet here we are in light probably brighter than it is outside. I don't understand it at all."

The Lama sighed, and said, "Let's have some food first, Lobsang, we are going to be here for several days and we could do with a change of diet. You go into that little room," he pointed, "and bring out some of those containers with pictures on them, and then we will see how the people of long, long ago used to live."

I rose to my feet and said to myself, "My, I know what I must do first. Honourable Lama," I said, "can I help you to attend to your body functions?" He smiled at me and replied, "Many thanks, Lobsang, but that is already attended to. There is a little place over there in that far corner, and if you go in there you will find there is a very convenient hole in the floor. Get over that hole and let Nature take its course!"

I went off in the direction to which he had pointed

and found the appropriate hole and made use of it. The room was of a glass-smooth surface and yet the flooring was not smooth, it was matt-like and one had no fear of slipping. Well, with that accomplished I thought of food again so I went into the room at the far end and carefully washed my hands because it was such a luxury to be able to turn a metal bar and find water would come out of a spout. I washed my hands thoroughly and turned off the tap, and then I felt a warm blast of air coming from a hole in the wall. It was a rectangular-shaped hole and it occurred to me that my hands would soon dry if I put them in that rectangular hole, and that is what I did and I think that was the best wash I ever had. The water was so pleasant, and I was keeping my hands in the hole when the heat went off. I suppose the designers allowed a certain amount of time in which people could reasonably be expected to dry off their hands. Then I went to the closet and opened the doors, and looked with bewilderment at the array of containers. There were all manner of containers with pictures, and the pictures were so strange that they meant nothing to me. For instance, a red thing with great big claws, it looked a ferocious monster and something, I thought, like an earwig. And then there were other pictures which showed what appeared to be spiders dressed in red armour. Well, I passed up those, and instead picked out some which had what was obviously fruit of some sort, some were red, some green, and others were yellow, and they all looked attractive. So I picked up as many as I could carry, and then I saw a trolley thing standing in the corner. It had wheels to it, and I put all these containers in and pushed the trolley thing out to the Lama Mingyar Dondup. He laughed like anything when he saw how I was managing, and he said, "And how did you like your hands washed? Did you like the method of drying them? Just think, that has been here for a few million years and it is still working because the atom which powers all this equipment is virtually indestructible, and when we leave everything will sigh to a stop, all the power will go back into storage and there it will wait until the next people come. Then the lights will come on again—the lights, by the way, are things which you would not understand because behind the glass-like surface there is a chemical which responds to a certain impetus by generating cold light. But let's see what you have brought."

I handed down the things to him, one by one, and he picked out four cannisters and said, "I think that will do us for now, but we shall want something to drink. In the cupboard above the water tap you will find containers that will hold water, so you fill two of those containers with water and in the bottom of the cupboard you will find another container with pellets inside. Bring one of those pellets and we shall have water of a different flavour."

Back I went into the—well—kitchen, and I found the containers just as described, and I filled them with water and took them out to the Lama. Then I went back and picked up a tube which held funny little tablets, they were orange coloured. So with that I went out again and the Lama took the container from me and did something to the top, and out popped a pellet straight into the glass of water. Then he repeated the performance, and a pellet popped out into the other glass of water. He then put one of the containers to his lips and had a hearty drink. I dubiously followed his example, and was surprised and delighted at the pleasant taste.

Then the Lama said, "Let's have some food before we drink any more." So he picked up one of the round containers and pulled on a little ring. There was a woosh of air. With that, as soon as the wooshing stopped, he pulled harder on the ring and the whole top of the container came off. Inside there were fruits. He smelt them carefully, then he took out one and put it in his mouth. "Yes, yes, they have kept perfectly, kept absolutely fresh. I will open one for you, pick which one you prefer and give it to me."

I looked at the things, and there were some black

fruit with little knobs all over them, so I said I would have that one. He pulled on a ring and again the woosh. Then he pulled harder and the entire top came off. But then there was a problem, these things inside were small and they were in liquid, so the Lama said, "We shall have to be more civilised. You go in and in one of the drawers you will find some pieces of metal which are dished at one end and they have a handle to them. Bring out two of them, one for you and one for me. By the way, they are metal and of a silvery colour."

Off I went again, soon to return with these peculiar bits of metal. "There are other things there, Master, bits of metal with spikes at one end, and others with what looks like a knife edge on one end."

"Oh yes, forks and knives, we will try them later on, but these things are spoons. Dip the end of a spoon in your cannister and you can ladle out fruit and juice, and then you can eat it or drink it without getting a mess all over yourself." He showed me by ladling out fruit from his container, so I followed his example and put the metal thing in the cannister to ladle out a small amount of the stuff. I wanted to taste a little first because I had never seen anything like this before.

"Ah!" It slid down my throat and left me feeling very gratified. I had not realised how hungry I was. Soon my cannister was empty. The Lama Mingyar Dondup was even faster. "We'd better go easy, Lobsang, because we've been out of food for quite a time.

"I do not feel able to walk about, Lobsang, so I suggest that you wander around looking at different compartments because we want to know all we can." Somewhat truculently I walked out of the big room and found that there were rooms all over the place. I went into one, the lights came on and the place seemed to be full of machinery which shone as though they had been installed only the same day. I wandered around nearly afraid to touch anything, but then quite by accident I came to a machine which was already showing a picture. It showed buttons being pressed and it was a moving picture, it showed a sort of a chair and a strange

45

looking man was helping an even stranger looking man to sit in the chair. And then the helping man took hold of two handles and I saw him twist the right-hand handle and the chair rose up several inches. Then the picture changed and showed the chair being pushed along to different machines, and doing things to them. It was doing it for me. I turned hurriedly and tripped over the wheeled chair, and fell flat on my face. My nose felt as if it had been knocked off and was all wet, so I had damaged my nose and it was bleeding. I pushed the chair in front of me and hurried back to the Lama. "Oh, Master, I tripped over this unmentionable chair and now I want a piece of something to wipe my bloody face."

I went to a box and unwrapped one of the blue-wrapped rolls. Yes, there was that peculiar white stuff inside like a lot of cotton bundled up together. After I had had it applied to my nostrils for several minutes the bleeding stopped, and I threw the bloody mess of cotton into a container which happened to be standing empty, and something impelled me to look in the container. I was shocked to see that the material just disappeared, not in the darkness or anything like that, but just disappeared. So I went over to the corner where I had swept all the puss and general muck, and with a flat piece of metal which had a wooden handle to it I picked up as much as I could at one go, and I dropped it in the refuse container where it all disappeared. Then I went to the far corner which of necessity we had used for our attention to the calls of Nature, and I scraped up everything that was there and put it in the container. Immediately all the stuff disappeared, and the container was looking shiny and new.

"Lobsang, I think that container should fit in that hole that we have been using, see if it will fit, will you?"

I trundled the thing in and—yes—it fitted perfectly into that hole, so I left it there ready for immediate use!

"Master, Master," I said in great excitement, "if you

will sit in this chair I can take you around and show you some absolute marvels." The Lama gingerly got to his feet and I slid the chair in under him. Then I twisted the handle as I had seen in the moving picture and the chair rose about a foot in the air, just the right height for me to hold the handles and steer the thing. So with the Lama Mingyar Donup in the, what I called wheeled chair which obviously depended on levitation and not wheels, we went back into that room with all the machinery.

"I think this was their entertainment room, Lobsang," said the Lama. "All these things are for playing games. Let's have a look at that box near the entrance to this room." So I turned about and pushed the chair back to the entrance, and I pushed the chair right up tight against the machine in which I had seen the chair-instructions. Once again I pressed a button and saw a moving picture. Of all incredible things it showed the Lama Mingyar Dondup getting into the chair and me pushing him in. And then we moved several feet in the room and the Lama was saying something so we turned around and went back to that machine. We saw all this which had just happened. Then the picture changed and it showed various machines, and it gave picture instructions about what they were. There was a machine near the centre of the room, and if one pushed a button there, various coloured small objects slid out into a tray, so we made our way there. The Lama pushed the indicated button, and with a metallic clatter some round things rolled out of a chute and into a little tray beneath the chute. We looked at the things, we tried to break them, and then I saw at the side of the machine a little dish thing with above it a curved blade. I put some of the round things in the container and pulled down on a handle—in fear and trembling—to see what would happen. The things were soon cut in half, and in them there appeared to be something gooey. I, always more or less thinking of food, touched one of the insides and then touched it against my tongue.

47

Ecstasy! The most wonderful taste I had ever had in my life. "Master," I said, "this is something you really must try." I wheeled him around to the button and he pressed again, and a lot more of these things came out. I took one and put it in my mouth, and it was just as if I had got a stone in my mouth. After a few moments, though, the outer shell of the thing became soft and my continued jaw pressure broke through the surface and then I got the sweetest of sweet tastes. There seemed to be different flavours. Each colour had a different flavour. Now I hadn't the faintest idea what this was, and the Lama saw I was at a loss. "I have travelled a lot, you know, Lobsang, and in a Western city I saw a machine like this, it had candy balls in it, the same as these are. But in that Western city one had to put money. One put a coin in a slot and so many of these balls would roll out. There were other machines like it, providing different things. There was one that appealed to me particularly because it had a stuff called chocolate in it. Now, I can't write the word for you. Ah! Ah!" he said, "There it is, there is that word written down here with six other words. I suppose they are all different languages. But let's see if this one works."

He pressed the button firmly, and the machine gave a little cough, and a door opened in the front. There we saw different types of chocolate or candies, and so we helped ourselves to so much that we felt heartily sick. I frankly thought I was going to die! I went to that disposal place and brought up all those things which I had eaten. The Lama Mingyar Dondup, abandoned in his chair, called for me to collect him in a hurry, so we will just draw a veil over the rest of that experience.

Recovered quite a lot, we discussed the matter and came to the conclusion that it was our greed which had made us eat too much of a strange food, so we moved into another room and this must have been a repair room. There were all manner of very strange machines, and I recognised one as being a lathe. The Dalai Lama had one in one of his storage rooms, it had been sent to him by a friendly nation who wanted to be friendlier still. Nobody knew how to use it, of course, but I sneaked into the room on many, many occasions and eventually was able to work out what the thing was. It was a treadle lathe. You sat on a wooden seat and you used your feet together to push two pedals up and down. That caused a wheel to rotate, and if one put, say, a piece of wood between what was labelled "head-stock" and "tailstock" one could carve the wood and make absolutely straight rods. I could not see what use it could be, but I took our staves and smoothed them off, and we felt so much better with what I could only call a professionally made stave.

We moved about and we saw a thing which appeared to be a hearth. There were blow pipes and all manner of heat-tools about, and soon we were experimenting. We found that we could join metals together by melting one piece onto another, and we spent much time trying out different things and improving our skills. But then the Lama said, "Let's look elsewhere, Lobsang, there are some wonderful things here, eh?"

So I twisted the handle again, and the wheeled chair rose about two feet. I pushed it out of the tool room and into a room right across a big space. Here was mystery indeed. There were a number of tables, metal tables, with huge bowls over them. It did not make any sense to us, but then in an adjoining room we found a recess into the floor and printed on the wall just above it there were obviously instructions on how to use the thing. Fortunately there were also pictures showing how to use it, so we sat down on the edge of the empty pool and took off the Lama's bandages. Then from the side I helped him to stand up, and immediately he stood in the centre of the pool it began to fill with a steaming solution!

"Lobsang, Lobsang, this is going to heal my legs. I can read certain of the words on the wall, and if I can't read it in one language I can in another. This is a thing for regenerating flesh and skin."

"But Master," I said, "how can that possibly heal

your legs, and how is it that you know so much about these languages?"

"Oh, it's very simple," he said, "I've been studying this type of thing for the whole of my life. I have travelled extensively throughout the world, and I have picked up different languages. You may have noticed that I have books always with me, and I spend all the time I have to spare reading these books and learning from them. Now, this language," he pointed to writing on the wall, "is what is called Sumrian, and this one was the main language of one of the Atlantises."

"Atlantises?" I thought, "But the place was Atlantis." I said so, and the Lama laughed at me quite gleefully and said, "No, no, Lobsang, there is no such place as Atlantis, it is a generic term for the many lands which sank beneath the ocean and all trace of the lands was lost."

"Oh," I said, "I thought Atlantis was a place where they had a very advanced civilization to the extent that it made us like country yokels, but now you tell me there was no one specific Atlantis."

He broke in on my speech and said, "There is so much confusion about it, and the scientists of the world won't believe the truth. The truth is this; once upon a time this world had just one land mass. The rest was water, and eventually, through the vibrations of the Earth such as earthquakes, the one land mass was broken up into islands, and if they were bigger islands then they were called continents. They gradually drifted apart so that many of these islands had people who had forgotten the Old Language, and they used their own family dialect as their standard language. Years ago there was no speech, everyone communicated by telepathy, but then some wicked people took advantage of knowing what everyone was communicating to everyone else, and so it became the custom that in communities the leaders of the communities devised languages which they would use when they did not want to use telepathy which anyone could pick up.

In time the language became used more and more, and the art of telepathy was lost except for a few people like some of us in Tibet. We can communicate by thought. I, as an illustration, have communicated with a friend at Chakpori and told him of my exact situation, and he replied to the effect that it was just as well to stay where we were because there were raging storms which would make it very difficult for us to descend the mountain side. As he said, what does it matter where we are so long as we are learning something, and I think we are learning a lot. But, Lobsang, this stuff seems to be working marvels on my legs. You look at them and you will actually see them healing."

I did look, and a most eerie sight it was. The flesh had been cut right down to the bone, and I thought the only thing to do would be to amputate his legs when we got back to Chakpori, but now this marvellous round bath thing was healing the flesh. As I watched I could see new flesh growing, uniting the gashes.

The Lama suddenly said, "I think I'll get out of this bath now for a time because it is making my legs itch so much that I shall have to do a dance if I stay here, and that would be something to make you laugh. So I am coming out, and I don't even want a hand." He stepped surely out of the bath, and as he did so all the liquid disappeared. There was no hole for it, no drain-pipe or anything like that, it seemed just to disappear into the walls and bottom.

"Look, Lobsang, here are some books with utterly fascinating illustrations. It shows how to do certain operations, it shows how to operate those machines outside. We must set to work to try to understand this because we may be able to benefit the world if this ancient, ancient science can be revived."

I looked at some of the books, and they seemed pretty gruesome to me. Pictures of peoples' insides, of people with the most fearful wounds one could imagine, wounds so bad that one could not even imagine them. But I decided I would stick to it and I would learn all

51

I could about the human body. But first I came to the firm conclusion that food was necessary. One can't exercise the brain without a supply of food, and I voiced my thoughts on the matter. The Lama laughed and said, "Just what I was thinking about. That treatment has made me ravenously hungry, so let's go in this kitchen place and see what there is. We are either going to have to live on fruit or we shall have to break one of our rules and eat meat."

I shuddered, and felt quite sick. Then I said, "But Master, how can we possibly eat the flesh of an animal?"

"But, good gracious me, Lobsang, the animals have been dead millions of years. We don't know how old this place is, but we do know that it is in remarkably good repair. It's better for us to eat some meat and live than just be purists and die."

"Master, how is this place in such a good condition if it is a million years old? It doesn't seem possible to me. Everything wears out, but this place might have been vacated yesterday. I just don't understand it, and I don't understand about Atlantis."

"Well, there is such a thing as suspended animation. In fact these people, the Gardeners of the Earth, were subject to illnesses just the same as we are, but they could not be treated and cured with the crude materials available on this Earth, so when a person was really ill and beyond the skill of the Gardeners on this Earth then the patients were encased in plastic after having the treatment of suspended animation. In suspended animation the patient was alive, but only just. A heartbeat could not be felt, and certainly no breath could be detected, and people could be kept in that state alive for up to five years. A ship came down every year to collect these cases and take the sufferer away for treatment in special hospitals in the Home of the Gods. When they were repaired they were as good as new."

"Master, how about those other bodies, men and women, each one in a stone coffin? I am sure they are dead, but they look alive and they look healthy, so what are they doing here, what are they for?"

"The Gardeners of the Earth are very busy people. Their overseers are even more busy, and if they wanted to know about the real conditions among the earthlings they just took over one of these bodies. Their own astral form entered one of these bodies, they are just cases really, you know, and activated the body. And then one could be a man of thirty, or whatever age suited, without all the bother and mess of being born and living a childhood and perhaps taking a job, and even taking a wife. That could lead to a lot of complications. But these bodies are kept in good repair, and always ready to receive a "soul" which would activate them for a time, and they would respond to certain stimuli and the body would be able to move under perfect control at the will of the new and temporary occupant of the body-case. There are quite a number of these what we call transmigration people about. They are here to keep a check on the humans and try to avert and redirect some of the violent tendencies of these people."

"I find this utterly fascinating and almost unbelievable. And how about the bodies on the top of the Potala, the ones that are encased in gold, are they to be used as well?"

"Oh dear me, no," said the Lama. "These are humans of a superior type, and when the body dies the ego moves on to higher realms. Some go to the astral world where they wait about, studying some of the people in the astral world, but I shall have to tell you more about this and about the realm of Patra. So far as I am aware it is only we Tibetan lamas who know anything about Patra, but it's too big a subject to be rushed. I suggest that we look around a bit because this is quite a large cave complex." The Lama moved away from me to put some books back on the shelves, and I said, "Isn't it a pity to leave such valuable books on shelves like this, would it not be better for us to take them back to the Potala?"

The Lama Mingyar Dondup gave me a peculiar look, and then he said, "I grow more and more amazed at how much you know at your very young age, and the Dalai Lama has given me full permission to tell you anything that I think you should know."

I felt quite flattered at that, but the Lama went on, "You were present at the interview with those English soldiers, one was called Bell, and the Dalai Lama was absolutely delighted that you did not tell even me about it, what was said, what was done. I deliberately pressed you, Lobsang, to try you out for keeping secrets, and I am very pleased with the way in which you have responded.

"In a few years Tibet will be conquered by the Chinese, they will strip the Potala of all the things that made it the Potala, they will take away the Golden Figures and just melt down those figures for the gold they contain. Sacred books and books of learning will be taken to Pekin and studied because the Chinese know that they can learn a lot from us, so we have places of concealment for the more precious things. You would not have found this cave except by the merest chance, and we are going to obliterate the side of the mountain so the merest chance cannot be repeated, and, you see, we have tunnels interconnecting for more than two hundred miles, and the Chinese could not travel in their four-wheeled machines, and they certainly could not travel on foot, whereas to us it is just a two days journey.

"In a few years Tibet will be invaded but not conquered. Our wiser men will go up into the highlands of Tibet and they will live underground in much the same way as the people who escaped before live in the hollow part of this world. Now, don't get excited because we are going to discuss these things. The Dalai Lama says there is no hurry for us to get back. I've got to teach you as much as I can about as many things as I can, and we shall rely upon these books a lot. To take them back to the Potala would merely be to put them

54

in the hands of the Chinese, and that would be a sorry fate indeed.

"Well, I think it is time for us to carry out a systematic search of this particular cave, and we will draw a map of the place."

"No need to, sir," I replied. "Here is a map in the minutest detail."

CHAPTER FOUR

The Lama Mingyar Dondup looked exceedingly pleased and he was even more pleased when I pointed out maps of several other caves.

I had been rummaging around on a shelf and marvelling that there was not a speck of dust anywhere, and the—well, I would call it a paper, but actually it was some substance like paper only very, very much finer. Our paper was all handmade stuff from papyri. But I picked up this pile of paper and saw that they were maps and charts. First there was a very small scale map showing an area of about two hundred and fifty miles, and then the tunnel was marked out with certain breaks in the line to show where it was no longer passable and one would have to get out of our own tunnel and look for the entrance to the other one. It was shown on the map all right but how many earth-quakes had made the map inaccurate, that was the problem. But then the next map was a chart of the cave in which we were now ensconced. It showed all the rooms, and I was amazed at the number of rooms, and the cupboards and rooms were all labelled but, of course, I couldn't read any of it. My Guide, though, could. We laid the map on the floor and lay down on our tummies while we looked at it.

"Lobsang," said the Lama, "you have made some remarkable discoveries on this trip, and it is going to count very heavily in your favour. I brought a young chela here once and he was quite afraid to even enter the cave. You see, the old hermit who fell to his death was actually the Keeper of the entrance, and now we shall have to build a fresh hermitage to guard the entrance."

"I think we hardly need a Guardian, sir," I said, "because the whole of the tunnel through which we entered is blocked apparently through the earthquake shaking a whole sheet of rock, and that slipped down to cover this entrance. Were it not for these maps we could be stuck here for ever."

The Lama nodded gravely, and got to his feet and walked along beside the shelves looking at the books, reading their titles. Then, with an exclamation of delight, he pounced on one book—oh, it was a massive thing, a great big fat book, looking as though it had just been made. "A dictionary, Lobsang, of the four languages used. Now we are well away." He picked the book up and again brought it to the floor. It needed the floor to take all the charts, the table would have been too small. But the Lama went rustling through the pages of the dictionary and then, making notes on the chart of our particular cave, he said, "Centuries and centuries ago there was a very high civilization, far higher than the world has reached since, but unfortunately there were more earthquakes and seaquakes, and some lands sank beneath the waves and, according to this dictionary, Atlantis is not just one sunken continent. There was one in the sea which they called Atlantic, and there was another one lower down in the Atlantic, it was a place where there were many high peaks and those peaks still protrude above the waters and now they are called islands. I can show you on the map just where it is."

He rustled around among the papers and then produced a great big coloured sheet of paper, then he pointed out the seas and the places where Atlantis had been. Then he continued, "Atlantis—the lost land, that is the real meaning of the word. It is not a name like Tibet or India, it is a generic term for the lost land, the land which sank without trace."

We maintained silence while we looked at those charts again. I was anxious to know how to get out of the place. The Lama was anxious to find certain rooms. At last he straightened up and said, "There, Lobsang, there. In that room there are wonderful machines which show us the past and right up to the present, and there is a machine which shows the probable future. You see, with astrology, for example, you can foretell what is going to happen to a country, but when it comes to foretelling one particular person, well, that takes a genius of an astrologer, and you had such a genius astrologer forecast your future, and it is quite a hard future indeed.

"Let us explore some of the other rooms first because we want to spend a long time in the machine room where the machines can show us what happened since the first people came to this world. In this world they have many peculiar beliefs, but we know the truth because we have been able to tap into the Akashic Record and the Akashic Record of Probabilities, that is, we can foretell accurately what will happen to Tibet, what will happen to China, and what will happen to India. But for the individual—no, the Record of Probabilities is very much probability, and not to be taken too seriously."

"Master," I said. "I am absolutely confused because all the things I have learned have taught me that there is dissolution; paper should crumble to dust, bodies should crumble to dust, and food, after a million years, well, that certainly should have crumbled to dust, and I just cannot understand how this place can be a million or so years old. Everything looks new, fresh, and I just cannot understand it."

The Lama smiled at me, and he said, "But a million years ago there was a much higher science than there is today, and they had a system whereby time itself could be stopped. Time is a purely artificial thing, and is used only on this world. If you are waiting for something very nice then it seems an awful long time that you have to wait for it, but if you have to go to a senior

Lama to have a good telling off—well, it seems no time before you are in front of him listening to his opinion of you. Time is an artificial thing, so that people can engage in commerce or in everyday matters. These caves are isolated from the world, they have what I can only call a screen around them, and that screen places them in a different dimension, the fourth dimension where things do not decay. We are going to have a meal before we explore further, and the meal will be of a dinosaur which was killed by hunters two or three million years ago. You will find it tastes quite good."

"But Master, I thought we were forbidden to eat meat."

"Yes, the ordinary persons are forbidden to eat meat. It is considered quite adequate that they live on tsampa because if one gorges oneself on meat then one's brains get clogged. We are having meat because we want the extra strength which meat alone can give, and anyway, we have very little meat, mostly we have vegetables and fruits. But you may rest assured that eating this meat will not harm your immortal soul." With that he got up and went into the kitchen store, and he came out with a big container which had a most horrible picture wrapped around it. It showed what I imagined to be a dinosaur and outlined in red was a marking showing what part of the dinosaur was in the canister. The Lama did some things to the canister, and it came open. I could see that the meat inside was absolutely fresh, it might have been killed that day it was so fresh. "We are going to cook this because cooked meat is much better than the raw stuff, so you'd better watch what I do." He did some queer things with some of the metal dishes, and then he tipped the contents of the canister into one of those metal dishes and slid it into what looked like a metal cabinet. Then he shut the door and turned some knobs so that little lights came on. He said, "Now, in ten minutes, that will be perfectly cooked because it is not cooked on the flame but it is heated from the inside to the outside. It is some system of rays which I do not profess to understand. But now we must look about for some suitable vegetables which will go well with meat."

"But however did you learn all this, Master?" I asked.

"Well, I have travelled quite extensively and I have picked up knowledge from the Western world and I see how they prepare a special meal on the seventh day of the week. I must confess that it tastes really good, but it needs vegetables, and I think we have them here."

He put his hands deep into a closet and pulled out a long canister. He put it on the work shelf and carefully studied the label, then he said, "Yes, here are the vegetables and we have to put them in the oven for five minutes cooking." At that instant one light went out. "Ah," said the Lama, "That is a signal, we must push these vegetables in now." So saying, he went to the oven thing, opened the door, and slid in the complete canister, and then he quickly shut the door. Then he adjusted some of the knobs on the top, and a different light came on.

"When all these lights go off, Lobsang, our meal will be perfectly prepared. So now we have to get plates and those other fearsome implements that you saw, sharp knives and metal things with little bowls at the end, and those other things which have four or five spikes at the end, they are called forks. I think you are going to enjoy this meal."

Just as he finished speaking the little lights flickered, dimmed, and were extinguished. "There you are, Lobsang. Now we can sit on the floor and have a good meal." He moved forward to the hot place which he called an oven, and carefully he slid aside the door. The smell was beautiful and I watched with the keenest anticipation as he took the metal dishes off the shelves. He ladled out a good portion of everything for me, and then not so much for himself. "Start in, Lobsang, start in. We've got to keep your strength up, you know."

There were dishes, different coloured vegetables, none of which I had ever seen before, and then this bigger dish with a big lump of dinosaur meat on it.

Cautiously I held the meat with my fingers until the Lama told me to use a fork to hold the meat, and showed me how. Well, I cut off a piece of the meat, looked at it, smelt it, and put it in my mouth. Quickly I rushed to the sink in the kitchen and got rid of the meat in my mouth. The Lama was roaring with laughter. "You're quite wrong in your thoughts, Lobsang. You think I am playing a trick on you but I am not. In some parts of Siberia the local people sometimes dig up a dinosaur which has been caught in the permafrost and frozen so solid that it might take three or four days to thaw. They eat dinosaur meat with the greatest of pleasure."

"Well, they can have my share of this with even greater pleasure for me. I thought I was poisoned! What vile stuff it is. I would just as soon eat my grandmother than that muck!" Carefully I scraped the last remnants of the meat from my plate, and then looking dubiously at the vegetables I thought I would try some. To my astonishment they tasted very, very good indeed. Mind you, I had never tasted vegetables before, all I had ever had to eat before this occasion was tsampa and water to drink. So now I had a goodly helping of everything until the Lama said, "You'd better stop, Lobsang, you've had a really big meal, you know, and you are not used to these vegetables. This first time they may keep you on the run, they will go through you like a purge and I will give you a couple of tablets which will calm your disturbed stomach."

I swallowed the wretched tablets and they seemed as big as pebbles. After I had swallowed the things the Lama looked and said, "Swallow them like that, eh? The usual way is to wash them down with a good drink of water. Have a go at it now, fill up your cup with water and that will wash away the powdery taste."

Once again I got to my feet and went into the kitchen, tottered into the kitchen would be a better explanation because never in my life having had vegetables or fruit—well, I could feel alarming churnings inside me, so alarming, in fact, that I had to put down my cup and rush—run all the way—to that little room with the hole in the floor. A couple more feet and I should have been too late. However, fortunately I reached that hole just in time.

I returned to the Lama and said, "There are many things really puzzling me, and I just cannot get them out of my mind. For example, sir, you say this place might be two million years of age, then how is it that the vegetables and the fruit are quite palatable?"

"Look, Lobsang," responded the Lama, "you must remember that this world is millions of years of age, and there have been many, many different types of people here. For example, about two million years ago there was a species of creature on the Earth and they were known as Homo Habilis. They came into our era by inventing the first tools of this particular cycle. You see, Homo Sapiens is what we are, and we are derived from that other Homo which I have just told you about.

"To try to make you understand a bit more, let me say that the world is like a garden, and all the buildings in the world are plants. Well, every so often the farmer will come along and he will plough his garden. That means that he will turn up the soil, and in so doing he will upset all the plants and the roots. They will be exposed to the air for a few minutes, and then as the plough comes over again they will be buried more deeply so that in the end no one could tell that there had been such-and-such a plant in that garden. It is the same with humans on the world; think of us as the plants. But the humans of different types are tried out and if they cannot manage to the satisfaction of the gardeners then catastrophes and disasters will be their lot. There will be mighty explosions and earthquakes, and every trace of humanity will be buried, buried deep beneath the soil, and then a fresh race of people will appear. And so the cycle will go on, just as the farmer ploughs under the plants so the gardeners of the world caused such disasters that every trace of the habitations is shattered.

"Every so often a farmer will be busy with his patch

of ground, and then he might spot something sparkling in the ground where he is digging, so he will bend over and pick it up, wondering what it is. And perhaps he will tuck it in the front of his robe to take home and show to his wife and perhaps to his neighbours. He might have dug up something which was buried a million or so years ago and now, with earthquakes, that piece of brilliant metal will have been brought to the surface.

"Sometimes a piece of bone will be discovered and the farmer will spend perhaps a couple of minutes wondering what sort of creature it came from because there have been some very queer creatures on this Earth. There have been women, for instance, with a purple skin and eight breasts aside just like a pregnant bitch. I suppose it would be quite useful to have the sixteen breasts, but that race died out because it was impractical. If the woman had given birth to a lot of children her breasts would have become so pendulous that she would hardly be able to walk without falling over, so that race died out. And then there was another race whose men were about four feet tall, none taller than that, and they were born horsemen, not like you who can hardly sit on the tamest pony we've got, but these were extremely bow-legged and they had no need for stirrups or a saddle, or anything like that; their natural body conformity seemed to have been designed especially for horse riding. Unfortunately the horse hadn't been "invented" at that time."

"But, sir," I said, "I cannot understand how we can be in a mountain, right inside a mountain, and yet we have good brilliant sunlight and plenty of heat. It baffles me, and I cannot think of any solution."

The Lama smiled as he often smiled at some of my statements, and he said, "These rocks which we call mountains have special properties, they can absorb sunlight, and absorb and absorb it, and then, if one knows how, we can get the sunlight released to any degree of brightness that we need. As the sun is shining more or less all the time on the top of the mountains, well, we are always storing up sunlight for when the sun has gone about her journey and is beyond our vision. It is not at all a magical thing, it is a perfectly ordinary natural occurrence like the tides in the sea— oh, I forgot you had never seen the sea, but the sea is a vast body of water, it is not drinkable because it comes from fresh water which has run down a mountain side and across the earth bringing with it all sorts of impurities and poisonous subjects, and if we tried to drink the water it would hasten our death. So we have to use some of the stored sunlight. It falls on a special sort of plate, and then a cold draught of air plays on the other side of the plate, then the light manifests itself as heat on one side and cold on the other. The result of that is that droplets of water form, born of the light from the sun, and the cold from the earth. That will be absolutely pure water called distilled water, and so we can catch it in containers and then we have plenty of fresh drinking water."

"But, Master, this business of having things a million or two million years old—well, I just cannot understand it all. The water for instance, we turned a metal thing and we got cold water which, obviously, had been put in a tank somewhere a million or so years ago. Well, how hasn't it evaporated? How can it possibly be drinkable after all these years? It's got me absolutely defeated. I know on the Potala roof the water tank would soon dry up, so how can this be a million years old?"

"Lobsang! Lobsang! You think we have a good science now, you think we know a lot about medicine and science, but to the outside world even we are just a bunch of uneducated savages. Yet we understand things that the rest of the world does not, the rest of the world is a materialistic group of people. This water might be a million or two million or three million years old in years, but until we came here and broke the seal and set everything working—well, it might have been just an hour or two before. You see, there is such a thing as suspended animation. We have heard a lot from other countries about people who have gone into a cataleptic trance for months, and there is one now which has already passed the year and a half mark, and the person looks none the worse for it, she looks no older, it is just—well, she is alive. We can't feel a heart beat, we can't get any breath on a mirror, so what is keeping her asleep and why is it not doing her harm? There are so many things to be rediscovered, all these things were commonplace in the days when the Gardeners came. Purely as an example, let me show you the room—here it is on the chart, look—where bodies were kept in a suspended life stage. Once a year two lamas would go and enter that room, and one by one they would take the bodies out of stone coffins and then examine the bodies carefully for any ills. If everything was all right they would walk the bodies up and down to make their muscles work again. Then, after we had fed the bodies a bit, would come the task of putting the astral body of a Gardener in the body taken from a stone coffin. It is a most peculiar experience."

"What, sir? Is it really a difficult thing to do?"

"Now look at you, Lobsang, telling me on the one hand that you can't believe such a thing, and on the other hand you are trying to find as much information as you can. Yes, it is a dreadful feeling. In the astral you are free to be whatever size it is most convenient to be, you might want to be very small for some reason, or you may want to be very tall and broad for some other reason. Well, you pick the right body and then you lay down beside it, and the lamas would inject a substance in the apparently dead body and gently they would lift you and put you face down on that body. Gradually, over a period of five minutes or so, you would disappear, you would get fainter and fainter, and then all of a sudden the figure in the stone coffin would give a jerk and sit upright and make some sort of explanation, "Oh, where am I? How did I get here?" For a time, you see, they have the memory of the last person to use that body, but within a matter of twelve hours the body that you had taken would appear to be absolutely normal, and would indeed be capable of all the things that you could do if you were on Earth in your own body. We do this because sometimes we cannot afford to risk damaging the real body. These simulacrum bodies, well, it doesn't matter what happens to them, they've only got to find someone with the right conditions about them and then we could put the body in a stone coffin and let the life force drift away to another plane of existence. People were never forced into it, you know, it was always with their full knowledge and consent.

"Later on you will inhabit one of these bodies for a year less a day. The day is because the bodies would only last three hundred and sixty-five days without having certain intricate things happen to it. So it is better to have the take-over to last a year less one day. And then—well, the body which you are still occupying would get into the stone coffin, shuddering at the coldness of it, and gradually your astral form would emerge from the substitute body and would enter your own body and take over all its functions, all its thoughts, and all its knowledge. And on that now would be superimposed all the knowledge that you had gained during the past three hundred and sixty four days.

"Atlantis used to be a great exponent of this system. They had a great number of these bodies which were constantly being taken over by some super person who wanted to get a certain bit of experience. Then, having got the experience, they would come back and claim their own body and leave the substitute for the next person."

"But Master, I am honestly puzzled indeed by this because if a Gardener of the World has all these powers then why cannot he just look east or west or south or north and see what is going on? Why all this rigmarole of occupying a substitute body?"

"Lobsang, you are being dim. We can't afford to have the real high personage damaged, we cannot have his body damaged, and so we provide him with a substitute body, and if an arm or a leg be taken off that's just too bad, but it does not hurt the high entity who took over the body. Let me tell it to you like this; inside one's head there is a brain. Now that brain is blind, deaf, and dumb. It can only go about animalistic procedures, and it has no real knowledge of what it feels like. For an illustration let us say that the very high entity So-and-So wanted to experience what it was like to be burned. Well, in his own body he would not be able to get down to the rough, crude vibrations necessary for one to feel the burn, but in this lower entity body—yes, burns can be felt, so the super-entity enters the substitute body and then the necessary conditions occur and perhaps the super-entity can get to know what it is like through the experience of its substitute. The body can see, the brain cannot. The body can hear, the brain cannot. The body can experience love, hatred, and all those sort of emotions, but the super-entity cannot so it has to get the knowledge by proxy."

"Then all these bodies are all alive and ready to be used by anyone who comes along?" I asked.

"Oh no, oh no, far from that. You cannot enter the entity into the body if it is for the wrong purpose. The super-entity must have an absolutely authentic good reason for wanting to take over a body, it cannot be done from his sexual interests or his money interests because they do not help in the advancement of anyone on the world. It usually happens that there is some task being done by the Gardeners of the World, it is a difficult task because being super brains they can't feel things, they can't see things, so they make arrangements for an appropriate number of them (the super brains) to take over a body and come down to Earth and pose as earthlings. I always say that the biggest trouble is the awful smell with these bodies. They smell like hot, rotting meat, and it might take one half day before one can overcome the nausea occasioned by such a take-over. So there really is no way in which a super-entity who possibly has gone wrong somewhere can victimise the substitute body. It can watch what others are doing, obviously, but nothing can be done which will harm the super-entity."

"Well, all this is a terrific puzzle for me because if a super-entity is going to wait until a body is perhaps thirty years of age what is going to happen about the Silver Cord? It's obvious that the Silver Cord is not just cut off, or I suppose the body-in-waiting would just decay."

"No, no, no, Lobsang," the Lama replied. "These substitute bodies have a form of Silver Cord which leads to a source of energy which keeps the way open for the body to be occupied. This is known in most religions of the world. The Silver Cord is by metaphysical means connected to a central source, and the people who look after these bodies can assess their condition through the Silver Cord, and they can add nourishment or take away nourishment, depending on the condition of the body."

I shook my head, baffled, and said, "Well, how is it that some people have the Silver Cord emerging from the top of the head while others have it emerging from the umbilicus? Does it mean that one is better than the other? Does it mean that the belly button exit for the cord is for those not so evolved?"

"No, no, not at all, it doesn't matter in the slightest where the Silver Cord emerges. If you were of a certain type you could have a Silver Cord emerging from, say, your big toe as long as the contact is made, that is all that matters. And as long as the contact is made and kept in good order the body lives on in a state of what we call stasis. That means that everything is still. The body organs are functioning at their very, very slowest, and throughout the whole of a year a body will consume less than one bowl of tsampa. You see, we have to do it that way or else we should be for ever traipsing along these mountain tunnels making sure that a body is being properly looked after, and if we had people come here to feed the bodies then it would actually do harm to the body because a person could live under statis for several million years provided it has the necessary attention. And that necessary attention can, and is, given by way of the Silver Cord."

"Then can a great Entity come down and have a look to see what sort of body the super one is going to occupy?"

"No," said the Lama. "If the Entity who is going to take over a body saw the body unoccupied he wouldn't dream of entering such an ugly looking thing. Look—come with me, and we will go into the Hall of Coffins." So saying he picked up his books and his staff, and rose to his feet rather shakily.

"I think we should look at your legs first, you know, because you appear to be in considerable pain."

"No, Lobsang, let's have a look at these coffins first, and then I promise you we will do my legs."

Together we walked along fairly slowly, the Lama consulting his chart every so often, and then at last he said. "Ah! We take the next turning left and the next turning left again, and there is the door which we must enter."

We trudged on up the path and turned to the left, and took the first turning left again. And there was the door, a great door looking as though made of beaten gold. As we approached a light outside the door flickered on and then steadied into constant light, and the door swung open. We went inside, and I stopped a moment taking in the rather gruesome sight.

It was a wonderfully appointed room with a lot of posts and rails. "This is for a newly awakened body to hang on to, Lobsang," said the Lama. "Most times they are a bit giddy when they are awakened, and it is rather a nuisance to have one just awakened fall flat on his face and mar his features so much that he cannot be used for some time. It upsets all one's arrangements, and then perhaps we have to get a different body and a different entity, and that makes a lot of extra work. None of us appreciate that in the slightest. But come over here and look at this body."

Reluctantly I went over to where the Lama beckoned. I wasn't fond of seeing dead bodies, it made me wonder why humans had such a short lifespan, short indeed when you know of a tree which is about four thousand years old.

I looked into the stone coffin and there was a nude man there. On his body he had a number of—well, it looked like needles with thin wires coming from them, and as I watched every so often the body would give a twitch and a little jump, a most eerie sight indeed. As I watched he opened sightless eyes and closed them again. The Lama Mingyar Dondup said, "We must leave this room now because this man is going to be occupied very, very soon, and it is disturbing for all of them if there are intrusions about." He turned and walked out of the room. I gave a last look around, and then I followed quite reluctantly because the people in the stone coffins, men and women, were quite nude and I wondered what a woman would be doing occupying one of these bodies. "I am picking up your thoughts, Lobsang," said the Lama, "why shouldn't a woman be used for some things? You must have a woman because there are some places where men cannot enter just as there are certain places where women cannot enter. But let us move a little more quickly because we do not want to delay the waiting super-Entity."

We moved a bit more quickly, and then the Lama said, "You seem to have quite a lot of questions, you know, why not ask them because you are going to be a super-Lama and you have to learn an incredible amount, things which are taught to about only one in a million of the priesthood."

"Well," I said, "when the super-Entity has entered the guest body what happens then? Does he rush out to get a jolly good meal? I'm sure I would!"

The Lama laughed and replied, "No, he doesn't rush anywhere, he is not hungry because the substitute body has been kept fed and well nourished, ready for immediate occupancy."

"I can't see the point of it, though, Master. I mean, a super-Entity one would think he would enter a body which had just been born instead of all this messing about with dead bodies which are like zombies."

"Lobsang, just think for yourself. A baby has several years before it learns a thing, and it has to go to a school, it has to be subject to parental discipline and that is a real time waster. It wastes perhaps thirty or forty years, whereas if the body can do all that and then come to these coffins, then indeed he is worth much more, he knows all the conditions of life in his own part of the world, and he doesn't have to spend years waiting and learning, and not being at all sure of what it is all about."

"I have had experiences already," I said, "and things that have happened to me—well, they don't seem to have any sense in them. Possibly I shall get some enlightenment before we leave this place. And, anyhow, why is it that humans have such a terribly short lifespan? We read about some of the Sages, the really wise people, and they seem to have lived one hundred, two hundred, or three hundred years, and still look young."

"Well, Lobsang, it is just as well to tell you now, I am over four hundred years of age, and I can tell you exactly why humans have such a terribly short life.

"Several million years ago, when this globe was in its infancy, a planet came very close and almost hit this world, in fact it was driven out of its orbit because of the anti-magnetic impulses from the other world. But the other planet did collide with a small planet which it shattered into pieces which are now known as the asteroid belt. We shall deal with that more extensively a bit later on. For the present let me tell you that when this world was in formation there were tremendous volcanoes all over the place, and they were pouring out gouts of lava and smoke. Now, the smoke rose up and formed heavy clouds all around the Earth. This world was not meant to be a sunshine world at all. You see, sunlight is poisonous, sunlight has deadly rays which are very harmful to a human being. Well, the rays are harmful to all creatures. But the cloud

71

cover made the world like a greenhouse, all the good rays could come through but the bad rays were shut out, and people used to live for hundreds of years. But when the rogue planet came so close it swept away all the clouds covering this Earth, and in the space of two generations people had a lifespan of three score and ten. In other words, seventy years.

"The other planet, when it collided and destroyed the smaller world to form the asteroid belt, spilled its seas onto this world. Now, we have water forming our seas, but this other world had a very different sort of sea, it was a petroleum sea, and without that collision this world would have had no petroleum products and that would have been a very good thing because nowadays drugs are taken from petroleum and many of the drugs are harmful things indeed. But there it is, we just have to live with it. In those early days all the seas were contaminated with the petroleum products, but in time that petroleum sank down through the seas and through the sea beds and it was collected in great rock basins, basins which were the result of volcanic influences under the sea bed.

"In time the petroleum will be quite exhausted because the type of petroleum available now is of a type harmful to Man, its combustion causes a lethal gas to be formed. That causes many, many deaths, and it also causes pregnant women to produce sickly children and even, in some cases, monsters. We shall see some of these very shortly because there are other chambers we are going to visit. You will be able to see all this in the third dimensional stage. Now, I know you are bursting to find out how photographs could be taken a billion years ago. The answer is that there are tremendous civilisations in this Universe, and in those days they had photographic equipment which could penetrate the deepest fog or the darkest darkness, and so photographs were taken. Then, after a time, the super-science people came to this Earth, and they saw people dying like flies, one could say, because if people can only live until seventy years of age that is very short indeed and does not give one the opportunity to learn as much as one should."

I listened with rapt attention. I found all this utterly fascinating, and in my opinion the Lama Mingyar Dondup was the cleverest man in Tibet.

The Lama said, "We here on the surface of the Earth know only half the world because this world is hollow, as many worlds are, as the Moon is, and there are people living inside. Now some people deny that the Earth is hollow, but I know it is from personal experience because I have been there. One of the biggest difficulties is that scientists all over the world deny the existence of anything which THEY did not discover. They say it is not possible for people to live inside the Earth, they say it is not possible for a person to live several hundred years, and they say it is not possible that the cloud coverage, when swept away, caused the lifespan to shorten. But it is actually so. Scientists, you see, always go by text books which convey information which is about a hundred years old by the time it reaches the classrooms, and places like this—this cavern where we are now—were put here specially by the wisest men who lived. The Gardeners of the Earth could get ill just the same as the native humans, and sometimes an operation was necessary, an operation which could not be performed on Earth, so the sufferer was put into a state of suspended animation and sealed up in a plastic case. Then the medical men in the caves would send special etheric messages for a hospital space ship, and the hospital space ship would quickly come down and take away the containers with the people who were ill sealed inside. Then they could either be operated upon in space or taken back to their home-based world.

"You see, it is easy to travel at a speed much in excess of light. Some people used to say, 'Oh, if you travel at thirty miles an hour it will kill you because the air pressure would blow out your lungs.' And then, when that was proved false, people used to say, 'Oh, Man will never travel at sixty miles an hour, it would kill them.' And then the next statement was that people would never travel at a speed faster than the speed of sound, and now they are saying nothing can ever travel faster than light. Light has a speed, you know, Lobsang. It is composed of the vibrations which, emanating from some object, has its impact upon the human eyes, and the human eyes see what the object is. But quite definitely, within just a few years, people will be travelling at many times the speed of light, as do the visitors here in their special space ships. The ship outside in the other chamber, that was just getting ready to take off when the mountain quaked and sealed the exit. And, of course, immediately that happened all the air in that chamber was exhausted automatically and the people aboard were in a state of suspended animation, but they had been in suspended animation so long that if we tried to revive them now they would probably be quite insane. That is because certain highly sensitive portions of their brains would have been deprived of oxygen, and without oxygen they die, and the person who has such a dead brain—well, they are not worth keeping alive, they are no longer human. But I am talking too much, Lobsang. Let's go and look at some of the other rooms."

"Master, I would like to see your leg first because we have here the means of healing it quickly and it seems wrong to me that you should suffer when, through this super-science, you can be cured very, very quickly."

"All right then, Lobsang, my budding doctor. Let us go back to the place of health, and we will have a look at my leg and see what we can do."

CHAPTER FIVE

We walked along the corridor which separated room from room outside the main chamber, and soon we came to the "medical health room." In we went, and on came the lights as bright as before. The place looked untouched, there was no sign that we had been there previously, no sign that our dustcovered feet had left tracks, it looked as if the floor had been newly polished and the metal fittings around the central pool newly burnished. We observed that just in passing, and it stirred in my mind a thought of more questions, but first of all, "Master, will you put your legs in the pool now, and then I will take off these bandages."

The Lama swung his legs into the pool and sat on the tiled edge. I got in, and unwound the bandages. As I got down near the flesh I felt sick—sick. The bandages here were yellow and thoroughly beastly looking. "Whatever is the matter with you, Lobsang? You look as if you have had too much strange food to eat."

"Oh, Master, your legs are so bad, I think we shall have to try to get monks come and carry you back to Chakpori," I said.

"Lobsang, things are not always what they seem. Take off all the bandage, take off all the wrappings, do it with your eyes shut if you like, or perhaps I should do it myself."

I got to the end of the bandage, and I found that I should not be able to take that off because it was stuck in a perfectly horrible, gooey, scabulous mess from which I recoiled. But the Lama reached down for the bundle of bandage and gave quite a tug, and the end came away with syrupy strings of something dangling from it. Without turning a hair he just tossed the bandages down on the flooring, and said, "Well now, I am going to press this valve and then the pool will fill. I had it turned off before because, obviously, we didn't want you undoing bandages when you are up to your waist in water. You get out of the pool and I will turn the water on faster."

I hastily clambered out, and took a look at those horrid legs. If we had been in Chakpori or somewhere like that I think both of them would have been amputated, and what a thing that would be for the Lama Mingyar Dondup, always travelling around to do good for someone. But as I looked slabs of stuff fell off his legs, slabs of bilious yellow and green material fell off his legs and floated on the surface of the pool. The Lama hitched himself a bit higher out of the water and then turned the valve on more so the water level rose and the floating material floated out through what I suppose was an overflow device.

He looked at the book again, and then made certain adjustments to a bunch of—well, I can only call them valves, they were different coloured valves, and I saw the water changing colour and there was a very medicinal odour on the air. I looked at his legs again, and now they were showing pink, pink like on a new-born baby. And then he hoisted his robe a bit higher, and went a bit further down the sloping bottom so that the heeling water went half way up his thighs. There he stood. Sometimes he would stand still, sometimes he would walk slowly around, but all the time the legs were healing. They went from an angry pink to a healthy pink, and at last there was no trace of the yellow scab, no trace at all, it had gone completely, and I looked up from his legs to take a look at the bandages I had taken off. I felt my scalp tingle; the bandages had gone, no trace of them, not a mark, they had just gone, and I was so shocked and astonished that involuntarily

I sat down forgetting I was in the water, medicated water at that. When sitting down in the lotus position, well, if one is doing it in water one should keep one's mouth shut, the taste was horrible! And yet it wasn't, it was pleasant. I found that a tooth which had been giving me some trouble since I fell sometime before ceased to trouble me, I could feel it in my mouth. I stood up quickly and spat over the edge of the pool, yes there was the tooth, it was cracked in half. Now it lay there in front of me, and I said to myself, "There! Blast you, now you go and ache as much as you like!"

As I looked at the tooth I saw an absolutely weird sight. The tooth was moving, moving towards the nearest wall, and as it touched the wall it disappeared. There I stood like a fool, dripping with water from my shaven scalp to my bare feet, trying to look at something that wasn't there.

I turned around to ask the Lama Mingyar Dondup if he had seen it, and he was standing over a certain place on the floor where the tiling was of different colour, and warm healing air was coming out of the floor and he was soon dry. "Your turn, Lobsang," said the Lama. "You look like a half-drowned fish, so you'd better come over here and get yourself dry."

Truth to tell I did feel like a half-drowned fish, and then I thought, well, how can a fish be half-drowned when it lives in water. So I asked the Lama how it could be, and his reply was, "Yes, it is perfectly true, one can take a fish from the water and its gills start to dry immediately. If you put it back in the water it will actually drown. We do not know the mechanism of it, but we know it to be a fact. But you look a lot better now you have been on that healing pad, you were looking worn out before and now you look as if you could run a hundred miles."

I went across and looked at his legs at closer quarters, and even as I looked the pinkness started to disappear and his legs soon returned to their ordinary natural colour, and there was no trace at all that only an hour before the flesh had been almost stripped from his bones. Here were his legs, healthy, fresh-looking, and I had been thinking how they would be amputated!

"Master," I said, "there are so many questions that I am almost ashamed to ask you for the answers, but I cannot understand how food and drink which has been here for endless years can still be quite fresh and quite potable. Even in our ice refrigerator meat gradually goes bad, so how can it be that this place, millions of years of age, can be as new as though it were built only yesterday?"

"We live in a peculiar age, Lobsang, an age where no man trusts another man. Sometime ago people in a white country absolutely refused to believe that there were black people and yellow people, it was just too fantastic to be believed, and then some people travelling to another country saw men on horseback. Now, they had never seen horses before, they did not know there was such a thing as a horse, so they fled, and when they went back to their own country they said they had seen a man-horse, a centaur. But even when it was known that horses were animals which could be ridden by men, still many people disbelieved it and they thought that the horse was a special sort of human changed into an animal's form. There are so many things like that. People will not believe that anything new can be, unless they themselves have actually seen it, touched it, and pulled it to pieces. Here we are reaping the fruits of a very, very high civilisation indeed, not one of the Atlantises because, as I told you, Atlantis is only the word for the disappearing land. No, these places go back far far beyond Atlantis, and there is an automatic means of stopping all development, all growth, until a human comes within a certain range. So if no human came here again this place would remain just as it is now, impregnable and without any signs of corruption or dissolution. But if people come and use the place as we have done, then after a number of such users the place would deteriorate, it would age. Fortunately we are in one which has been very, very

78

rarely used, in fact it has been used only twice since it was made."

"Master, how can you possibly tell that only twice has this place been used?"

The Lama pointed up to something dangling from the ceiling. "There," he said, "if anyone passes beyond that it shows in figures, and this one shows the figure 3. The last one is you and me. When we leave, and it won't be for three or four days, the time of our stay will be recorded ready for the next people to enter and to speculate upon who was here before them. But you know, Lobsang, I am trying to get you to realise that the degree of civilisation when this place was built was the highest which has ever been attained on this world. You see, first of all they were the Guardians of the World, the Gardeners of the World. Their civilisation was such that they could melt rock—even the hardest rock—and leave it with a glasslike finish, and the melting would be what we term a cold melt, that is, no heat would be generated. So a place could be used immediately."

"But I really cannot understand why these so highly civilised people should want to live inside mountain ranges. You told me that this mountain range extends all the way across the world, and so why should they hide themselves?" I asked.

"The best thing we can do is to go to the room of the past, the present, and the future. This is the store of knowledge of all that has happened in the world. The history you have learned in classes is not always true, it has been altered in its recording to suit the king or dictator in power at the time. Some of these people want to be known as their reign being of the the Golden Age. But seeing the actual thing, the actual Akashic Record—well, then one can't go wrong."

"Did you say the Akashic Record, Master? I thought that we could only see that when we were in the astral plane. I did not know that we could come to the mountains and see all that had happened," I said.

"Oh yes, you forget that things can be copied. We have reached a certain stage of civilisation, we think we are shockingly clever and we wonder if anyone will ever be cleverer, but come along with me and I will show you the actual truth. Come along, it is quite a little walk, but the exercise will do you good."

"Master, isn't there some way that I can avoid you walking? Isn't there something like a sled? Or could I pull you if you were sitting on a stout piece of cloth?"

"No, no thank you, Lobsang, I am quite capable of walking the distance, in fact that exercise may be good for me as well. So let us set out."

We did "set out" and I should have liked to investigate some of the interesting things. I was vastly intrigued with the doors, each with an inscription engraved on the door itself. "All these rooms, Lobsang, are devoted to different sciences, sciences which have never yet been heard of on this world because here we are like blind people trying to find the way, in a house with many corridors. But I am as a sighted person because I can read these inscriptions and, as I told you, I have had experience of these caves before."

At last we came to an apparently blank wall. There was a door to the left, and a door to the right, but the Lama Mingyar Dondup ignored them and instead he stood right in front of that blank wall and uttered a most peculiar sound in an authoritative tone. Immediately, without a sound, the blank space split down the middle and the two halves disappeared into the sides of the corridor. Inside there was just a faint light showing, a glimmering as of starlight. We went in to the room and it seemed as large as the world.

With a very slight sigh the two halves of the door slid across the corridor and this time we were at the opposite side of the apparently blank wall.

The light brightened somewhat so that we could dimly see a great globe floating in space. It was more pear-shaped than round, and there were flashes from both ends of the globe. "These flashes are the magnetic fields of the world. You will learn all about that a bit later."

I stood with mouth agape, there seemed to be shimmering curtains of ever-changing light around the poles, they seemed to undulate and flow from one end to the other, but with a very great weakening of colours round about the equator.

The Lama said some words, words in a language unknown to me. Immediately there came the light of faint dawn, like the light which comes at the birth of a new day, and I felt like one who had just sat up now awakened from a dream.

But it was no dream, as I soon found. The Master said, "We will sit over here because this is a console with which the ages of the world can be varied. You are not in the third dimension now, remember, here you are in the fourth dimension, and few people can live through that. So if you feel in any way upset or ill then tell me quickly and I can put you right."

I could dimly see the Lama's right hand reached out and ready to turn a button. Then he turned to me again and said, "Are you sure you feel all right, Lobsang? No feeling of nausea, no feeling of sickness?"

"No, sir, I feel just fine and absolutely fascinated, and I am wondering what we shall see first."

"Well, first of all we have to see the formation of the world, and then the arrival of the Gardeners of the World. They will come and look around, survey the place and all that, and then they will go away to plan, and later still you will see them arrive in a huge spaceship because that is really what the Moon is."

Suddenly all was dark, the darkest darkness that I had ever experienced, even on a moonless night there had been dim starlight, and even in a closed room with no windows there was still an impression of a little light. But here there was nothingness, not a thing. And then I nearly jumped off my seat, I nearly jumped out of my robe with fright; with incredible speed two faint dots of light were coming together, and they hit, they collided, and then the screen was filled with light. I could see swirling gases and smokes of different colours, and then the whole screen, the whole globe filled everything. I could see rivers of fire running down from flame-belching volcanos. The atmosphere was almost turgid. I was aware, but dimly, that I was watching something and that I wasn't actually there in person. So I watched and was more and more fascinated as the world shrank a little and the volcanos became less, but the seas were still smoking with the hot lava which had poured in. There was nothing except rocks and water. There was only one stretch of land, not a very large stretch of land, but just one solid lump, and it gave to the globe a peculiar erratic motion. It did not follow a circular path but seemed to be following a path which some shaky child had drawn.

Gradually as I watched the world became rounder and cooler. Still there was nothing but rock and water, and terrible storms which raged across the surface. The wind pushed over the tops of mountains, and those tops fell down the mountain sides and were ground into dust.

Time elapsed, and by now the Earth covered part of the world because the Earth itself was made by the ground up dust from the mountains. The land heaved and shook, and from certain parts there came great gouts of smoke and steam, and as I watched I saw a section of land suddenly break off from the main continental mass. It broke off and for seconds it seemed to hang on to the main mass in a vain hope of being reunited. I could see animals slithering down the sloping banks and falling into the steaming water. Then the broken piece cracked more, it broke off completely and disappeared beneath the waves.

Somehow I found that I could see the other side of the world at the same time, and I saw, to my unutterable amazement, land rising out of the sea. It rose up like a giant hand rising it, it rose up, shook a bit, and then quivered to a standstill. This land, of course, was just rock, not a plant, not a blade of grass, and nothing like trees. And then, as I watched, a mountain nearby burst into flames, lurid flames, red, yellow and blue, and then there came a flow of lava, white hot, flowing like a stream of hot water. But as soon as it touched the water it jelled and solidified, and soon the surface of the bare rock was covered by a rapidly cooling mass of the yellow-blue.

I looked up in wonder, and I wondered where my Guide had gone. He was there just behind me, and he said, "Very interesting, Lobsang, very interesting, eh? We want to see a lot more so we will skip the bit where the barren earth shook and writhed under the cooling by space. When we return we shall see the first types of vegetation."

I sat back in my chair, and I was absolutely amazed. Was this really happening? I seemed to be a God looking down at the birth of the world. I felt "peculiar" because this world in front of me seemed larger than the world I knew, and I—well, I seemed to be possessed of remarkable powers of vision. I could see the flames eating out the centre of the world so that it would be a hollow world, something like a ball, and all the time as I watched there fell upon the surface of the Earth meteorites, cosmic dust, and strange, strange things.

Before me, quite within my touch, I thought, there fell some machine. I could not believe this at all because the machine was ripped open and bodies fell out, bodies and machinery, and I thought to myself, "In some future Age someone might come across this wreckage and wonder what caused it, wonder what it was." My Guide spoke, "Yes, Lobsang, that's already been done. In this present Age coalminers have come across truly remarkable things. Artefacts of a skill unknown on this Earth, and then also there has come to light in coal some very strange instruments, and in one case the complete skeleton of a very tall, very big man. You, Lobsang, and I are the only ones to see this because before the machine was quite completed the Gods known as the Gardeners of the World had quarrelled over women, and so we can only see the formation of this, our Earth. If the machine had been completed we would have been able to see on other worlds as well. Wouldn't that have been a marvellous thing?!"

The meteorites rained down raising splashes of water when they touched that liquid, and causing bad indentation when they hit rock or the rudimentary soil which at that time covered the Earth.

The Lama moved his hand to another button—switches, I suppose they were really called—and the action speeded up so fast that I could not see what it was, and then it slowed down again. I saw a lush surface on the world. There were vast ferns larger than trees towering up toward the sky, the sky now covered with purple cloud, and causing the air itself to be of a purple hue. It was fascinating at first to see a creature breathing in and then exhaling what looked like purple smoke. But I soon got tired of that, or soon got accustomed to it, and I looked further. There were ghastly monsters, incredible things which trod their stolid way through marshlands and bog. It seemed as if nothing could stop them. One vast creature—I haven't the vaguest idea what it was called—came across a whole group of slightly smaller creatures. They would not move, and the larger one would not stop so he just lowered his head and with a massive spike of bone on what I suppose was his nose he just ripped his way through the other animals. The damp soil was strewn with blood, intestines, and other things of a like nature, and as these parts of the animals fell to the ground there emerged from the water peculiar things with six legs and jaws shaped like two shovels. These things tucked in to all the food they found, and then looked about them for more. Yes, there was one of their members who had fallen over a log, or something, and broken a leg. The others all set upon him and ate him alive, leaving only the bones to bear evidence of what had happened. But soon the bones were covered with foliage which had grown, flourished and withered, and fallen to the ground. Millions of years later this would be a coal seam and the bones of the animal would be dug up and be a seven day wonder.

The world spun on, faster now because things were developing more quickly. The Lama Mingyar Dondup stretched out to another switch and with his left elbow he jabbed me in the ribs and said, "Lobsang, Lobsang, are you sure you are not asleep? This you must see. Now stay awake and watch." He switched on whatever it was, it might be called a picture but it was three dimensional, one could get behind it without any apparent effort. The Lama dug me in the ribs and pointed up at the purple sky. There there was the gleam of silver, a long silver tube closed at both ends was slowly descending. At last it was clear of the purple clouds, and it hovered many feet above the land, and then, as though it had come to a sudden great decision, it dropped gently to the surface of the world. For a few minutes it just stayed there, motionless. One had the impression of some wary animal looking about before leaving the safety of its covering.

At last the creature seemed to be satisfied, and a great section of metal fell from the side and hit the ground with a soggy clang. A number of peculiar creatures appeared in the opening and looked about them. They were about twice the height of a tall man, and twice as broad, but they seemed to be covered in some sort of garment which covered them from head to foot. The head part was quite transparent. We could see the stern, autocratic faces of the people inside. They seemed to be poring over a map and making notations as they did so.

At last they decided that everything was all right, and so one by one they dropped on to the big piece of metal which had fallen to the ground but which yet remained attached to the vessel by one side. These men were covered in some sort of sheath or protective clothing. One of the men—I guessed that they were men although it was hard to say through all the smoke and the difficulty of seeing past their transparent head-

85

pieces—but one of them stepped off the big sheet of metal and fell flat on his face in the murk. Almost before he had touched the surface vile looking creatures dashed out of the vegetation and attacked him. His comrades lost no time in producing some sort of a weapon from the belt they wore. Quickly the man was pulled back onto the sheet of metal, and it was seen that the covering of the body was badly torn, apparently by animals, and red blood was flowing. Two of the men carried him aboard the ship, or whatever it was, and several minutes later they came out again carrying something in their hands. They stood on the metal sheet and both pushed a button on an instrument that they were carrying, and flame came out from a pointed nozzle. All the insect things on the sheet curled up into a burned crisp, and were swept off the metal sheet which then closed up into the body of the ship.

The men with the flames moved cautiously around playing the flames on the floor or on the ground, and burning quite a swathe of earth on one side of the ship. Then they switched off their flames and hurried after the other men who had gone through a forest of ferns. These ferns were as big as big trees, and it was easy to follow the passage of men through them because apparently they had some sort of cutting device which just swung from side to side and cut the fern down almost to ground level. I decided I must try to see what it was they were doing.

I moved from my seat and went a little way left. There I got a better viewpoint because now I could see the men apparently coming toward me. In front of the other men two men held some machine which glided along and cut down all the fern that got in its way. It seemed to have a rotating blade, and soon they broke through the forest of fern and found an open space in which a number of animals were gathered. The animals looked at the men and the men looked at the animals. One man thought he would test their aggressiveness so he pointed a metal tube at them and pulled on a little spur of metal. There was a tremendous explosion, and the animal at which the weapon had been pointed just fell to pieces, just collapsed. It reminded me of a monk who had fallen from the top of a mountain, everything was so scattered. But of the other animals there was no sign, they took off too quickly.

"We'd better move on a bit, Lobsang, we've got a lot of ground to cover and we will speed up for about a thousand years." The Lama moved one of those switch knobs, and everything in the globe swirled around like a whirlpool, and eventually it came to its natural rate of rotation.

"This is a more suitable time, Lobsang. You'd better observe carefully because we will see how these caves were made."

We looked very carefully and we saw a very low ridge of hills, and as they revolved closer to us we saw that it was rock, rock covered in green mossy material, except for the very top, and that top just showed bare rock.

Off to one side we saw some strange houses, they seemed to be half round. If you cut a ball in half and you put the half that has been cut on the ground then you would have some idea of what these buildings were like. We looked at them and saw people moving about. They were clad in some material which clung to their bodies and left no doubt as to which sex was which. But now they had the transparent headpiece off, and they were talking to each other and there seemed to be quite a lot of quarrelling going one. One of the men was apparently the chief; he brusquely gave some orders and a machine came out of one of the shelter places and moved toward the rocky ridge. One of the men moved forward and sat on a metal seat at the back of the machine. Then the machine moved forward, emitting "something" from nozzles all along the front, the forward part, the bottom and the sides, and as the machine moved slowly forward the rock melted, and seemed to shrink inside itself. The machine emitted ample light so we could see it was boring a tunnel right into the living rock. It moved on and on, and then it started to circle and in the space of a few hours it had excavated the big cave into which we first entered. It was an immense cave, and we could see that it was really a hutment or hangarage for some of their machines which were flying about all the time. It all seemed most puzzling to us. We forgot all about time, we forgot all about being hungry or thirsty, and then, when the great chamber was finished, the machine followed a path which had apparently been marked on the floor and that path was converted into one of the corridors. It went on and on and on, out of our sight, but then other machines came in and in the corridors they excavated rooms of different sizes. They seemed to melt the rock. It seemed just to melt and then push its way back leaving a surface as smooth as glass. There was no dust and no dirt, just this gleaming surface.

As the machines did their work, gangs of men and women moved into the rooms carrying boxes and boxes and more boxes, but the boxes all seemed to float in the air. Certainly they were no effort to lift. But an overseer stood in the centre of a room and pointed to where each box should be deposited. Then when the room had its full complement of the boxes the workers started unpacking some of them. There were strange machines and all manner of curious objects, one I recognised as being a microscope. I had seen a very crude one before because at one time the Dalai Lama had been given one from Germany, and so I knew the principal of the thing.

We were attracted by a brawl which seemed to be taking place. It was as if some of the men and women were opposed to the other men and women. There was much shouting, must gesticulation, and at last a whole collection of men and women got into some of these vehicles which travelled through the air. They said no goodbyes or anything like that, they just got inside and a door was closed, and the machines went up into the air.

A few days later—the days according to the speed of the globe we were watching—a number of the ships came back, and they hovered above the encampment. Then the bottom of the ships opened and things fell out. We looked and we could see people running with desperate speed away from where the things would fall. Then they threw themselves flat on the ground as the first object hit the ground and exploded in a violent brilliant flash of purple. We had difficulty in seeing because we were absolutely dazzled by the brilliant flash, but then from the forest of ferns there came thin shafts of brilliant light. They moved about, and one of the shafts struck one of the machines in the air. Immediately it vanished in a burst of flame.

"You see, Lobsang, even the Gardeners of the Earth had their problems, their problems were sex, there were too many men and too few women, and when men have been away from women for a long time—well, they get lustful and they resort to great violence. There is no point in us watching this because it is just a case of murder and rape." After a time a lot of the ships departed, apparently to their mother ship which was circling the globe far out in space. After some days a number of big ships came and landed, and heavily armoured men came out and they started hunting their fellows through the foliage. Whoever they saw they shot without asking any questions, shot, that is, if the person was male. If she was female they captured her and carried her off to one of the ships.

We had to stop. The pangs of hunger and thirst were pressing too much. So we had our ordinary tsampa and water, and having got through that and done a few other things we returned to the chamber which had the globe which appeared to be the world. The Lama Mingyar Dondup switched on something, and we saw the world again. There were creatures on it now, creatures about four feet tall and very, very bandy. They had weapons of a sort consisting of a piece of stick at one end of which was lashed a sharp stone which they made sharper by chipping away and chipping away until there was a really sharp edge. There were a number of the men making these weapons, and others were making weapons of a different kind. They seemed to have a strip of leather, and in it they placed large stones. Two men drew back the leather loop which was saturated in water to make it stretchable, and they together released the loop. A stone would go soaring away towards the enemy.

But we were more interested in seeing how civilisations changed, so the Lama Mingyar Dondup worked his controls again and everything became obscure in the globe. It seemed to be several minutes before there was a gradual lightening as of the dawn slowly appearing, and then there was normal daylight again and we saw a mighty city with tall spires and minarets. From tower to tower there stretched flimsy looking bridges. It was a marvel to me that they could support themselves let alone take traffic, but then I saw that all the traffic was aerial traffic. Of course, a few people walked about on the bridges and on the different levels of street, but then all of sudden we heard a thunderous roar. It did not dawn on us for a moment that it came from the three dimensional globe, but we looked intently and we could see minute specks coming towards the city. Just before reaching the city the minute specks circled and dropped things from their undersides.

The mighty city collapsed. The towers were shorn off, the bridges crumpled up like pieces of string too knotted and twisted to be of any use.

We saw bodies falling out of the higher buildings. We guessed they must have been the leading citizens because of their dress and because of the quality of the furnishings which fell with them.

We looked on dumbly. We saw another lot of little dark dots coming from the other direction, and they engaged the invading dots with unparalleled ferocity. They seemed to have no regard at all for their own life, they would shoot things at the enemy and if that failed to bring them down then the defenders would dive direct on to these—well, I can only call them big bombers.

The day ended and night fell upon the scene. The night lightened by mighty flares as the city burned. Flames were breaking out everywhere, from the other side of the globe we could see cities there in flames, and when the light of an early dawn shone upon the scene with the blood-red sun following on we saw just heaps of wreckage, just piles of dust, and distorted metalwork.

The Lama Mingyar Dondup said, "Let us skip a bit, we don't want to see all this, Lobsang, because you, my poor friend, will be seeing this in actual life before your span on this world is terminated."

The globe that was the world spun on. Darkness to light, light to darkness, I forgot how many times the globe spun, or perhaps I never did know, but at last the Lama put out his hand and the swirling globe slowed to its normal rate.

We looked carefully this way and that way, and then we saw men with bits of wood in the shape of a plough. Horses were dragging the ploughs through the ground, and we saw building after building just topple, topple into the trench dug by the plough.

For day after day they went on with their ploughing until there was no sign that there had ever been a civilisation in this area. The Lama Mingyar Dondup said, "I think that is enough for today, Lobsang, our eyes will be too tired to do anything tomorrow, and we want to watch this because this is going to happen time after time until, in the end, battling warriors will almost exterminate all life on the world. So let us just get some food and retire for the night."

I looked up in surprise. "Night, Master?" I said, "But how do we know what time it is?" The Lama pointed to a little square a fair way off the ground, perhaps as tall as three men standing on each others shoulders. There was a hand there, a pointer, and on what appeared to be a tiled background there were certain divisions of light and darkness, and the hand now was pointing between the lightest light and the darkest dark. "There you are, Lobsang," said the Lama, "a new day has almost started. Still, we have plenty of time to rest. I am going to stand in the fountain of youth again because my legs are hurting quite a bit, I think I must have scraped the bone very badly as well as lascerating the flesh."

"Master, Master," I said, "let me attend to it for you." I sped into the room of the fountain and hoisted up my robes. Then the water started to come, and I moved the little thing which the Lama had called a tap, I moved it so that the water kept on flowing after I got out, and I turned another tap thing which I had been told admitted a lot of medicated paste into the water where it rapidly dissolved and swirled around with the water.

The Lama sat on the edge of the pool, and then swung his legs over and into the water. "Ah!" he said, "That feels better. This brings great relief, Lobsang, soon my legs will be quite normal again and this will be just something to talk over with wonder."

I rubbed his legs briskly, and little bits of scar tissue came off until at last there was no scar tissue left and his legs again looked normal. "That looks better, sir," I said. "Do you think you have had enough for now?"

"Yes, I am sure I have. We don't want to keep at it half the night do we? We will make that do for now and go in search of food." So saying he climbed out of the pool and I turned the big wheel thing which let all the water flow away somewhere. I watched until the basin was quite empty, and then I turned on the tap full just to flush away bits of scar tissue. With that gone I turned the taps off again and went in search of the Lama.

"We've done enough for today, Lobsang," said my Guide. "I vote that we have tsampa and water for our supper, and then we go to sleep. We will eat better in the morning."

So we sat down on the floor in the usual lotus position, and we spooned out the tsampa. Now we felt ultra-sophisticated, we were not taking our tsampa scooped up by our fingers, we were using a civilised implement which, by the illustration in one of the books, was called a spoon. But before I could finish my supper I fell over backwards, dead to the world again, sound asleep, and the world rolled on and on.

CHAPTER SIX

I sat up suddenly in the darkness, wondering wherever I was. As I sat up the light came on gradually, not like lighting a candle where you get darkness one moment and a glimmer of light the next, this came on like the dawn, so there was no strain to the eyes. I could hear the Lama Mingyar Dondup pottering about in the kitchen. He called out to me and said, "I am preparing breakfast for you, Lobsang, because you will have to eat stuff like this when you move to the Western part of the world, just as well to get used to it now," and he laughed with secret glee.

I got up and started to make my way to the kitchen. Then I thought, no, Nature comes first, and so I reversed my direction of travel so that Nature COULD come first.

With that safely accomplished I went back to the kitchen and the Lama was just putting some stuff on a plate. It was a sort of brownish-reddish stuff, and there were also two eggs, fried, I suppose they were, but in those early days I had never before eaten fried food. So he got me sitting at a table and he stood behind me. "Now, Lobsang, this thing is a fork. You take the fork in your hands and hold down the piece of bacon while you cut it with the knife held in your right hand. Then, having cut it in half, you use the fork to convey the piece of bacon to your mouth."

"What a darn stupid idea," said I, picking up the bacon with finger and thumb and thereby getting a rap across the knuckles from the Lama.

"No, no, no, Lobsang. You are going to the West on a special task, and you've got to live as they live, and for that you've got to learn how to do it now. Pick up that bacon with your fork and convey it to your mouth, and then put it in your mouth and withdraw the fork."

"I can't, sir," I said.

"Can't? And why cannot you do as I say?" the Lama asked.

"Well, sir, I had that stuff to my mouth and you gave me a rap across the knuckles which made me let go, so I've eaten the wretched stuff."

"You have the other half there, look. Pick it up with your fork and convey it to your mouth. Put it well inside your mouth and then withdraw the fork."

So I did that, but it did seem such a stupid idea. Why should anyone have to have a bit of bent metal to convey food to his mouth? It was about the craziest thing I had heard, but here was even worse; "Now work the concave part of the fork under one of those eggs, and then cut with the knife so that you have about a quarter of the egg on the fork. You then put it to your mouth and eat it."

"Do you mean to say that if I go to the West I've got to eat in this crazy fashion?" I asked the Lama.

"I certainly do mean that, so its just as well for you to get used to it now. Fingers and thumbs are very useful for a certain grade of people, but you are supposed to be superior material. What do you think I am bringing you to a place like this for?"

"Well, sir, we fell in the wretched place by accident!" I said.

"Not so, not so," said the Lama. "We came in by accident, yes, admittedly so, but this was our destination. You see, the old hermit was the Keeper of this place. He had been the Keeper for about fifty years, and I was bringing you to expand your education a bit. But I think that fall on the rock must have knocked all your brains out."

"I wonder how old these egg things are," said the Lama thoughtfully. He put down his knife and fork, and went to the container where the eggs were kept, and I saw him counting noughts. "Lobsang, these eggs and this bacon are about three million years old, and they taste as fresh as if the eggs had been laid only yesterday."

I played about with the egg and the rest of the bacon. I was puzzled. I had seen things decay even when packed in ice, and now I was told I was eating stuff about three million years old. "Master, I have so many puzzlements, and the more you tell me the more questions you raise in my mind. You say these eggs are about three million years old, and I agree with you, they really are like fresh laid eggs, no trace of deterioration, so how is it possible for these to be three million years old?"

"Lobsang," said the Lama, "it would need a very abstruse explanation to really satisfy you about certain of these things, but let us look at it in a way which is not strictly accurate but which should give you some idea of what I mean. Now, supposing you have a collection of blocks. These blocks, we will call them cells, can be assembled to form different things. If you were playing as a child you could make block houses from these little cubes, and then you could knock over your house and make something quite different. Well, bacon, eggs or anything else, is composed of little blocks, little cells which have unending life because matter cannot be destroyed. If matter could be destroyed the whole Universe would come to a halt. So Nature arranges that these particular blocks are made into a shape which represents bacon, and those particular blocks represent eggs. Now, if you eat the bacon and the eggs you are not wasting anything because eventually all this passes through you, undergoing chemical changes on the way, and eventually it gets out to the land, or the earth, where it nourishes newly growing plants. And then perhaps a pig or a sheep will come along and eat the plants, and grow bigger. So everything depends on these blocks, these cells.

"You may get cells which are oval, and we will say

that is the natural type of cell. It enables a person to be built who is shapely, slender, and perhaps tall. That is because the cells, the oval cells are all laid in one direction. But supposing we get a man who loves to eat, who eats far more than he should because one should eat only enough to satisfy one's immediate hunger. But, anyway, this man eats for the love of eating, and his oval cells turn into round cells, the round cells are round because they have been filled up with excess food in the shape of fat. Now, of course, when you get an oval it has a certain length, and then if you make it into the round without increasing its capacity it is of a slightly less length, and so your fat man is shorter than he would be as a thin man."

I sat back on my heels and thought it all out, and then I said, "But what is the good of all these cells unless they contain something which gives life and which makes one able to do something which another person cannot do?"

The Lama laughed at me and replied, "I was giving you a very rough illustration only. There are different sorts of cells. If you get one sort of cell and it is treated properly you might be a genius, but if you get that same sort of cell and you treat it badly then you might be a madman. I am beginning to wonder which you are!"

We had finished our breakfast in spite of the injunction that one should not talk while one is eating. Attention should be paid to the food otherwise it was disrespectful. But I supposed that the Lama knew what he was doing, and perhaps he had special permission to break a few of our laws.

"Let's look about a bit. There are all kinds of strange things to see here, you know, Lobsang, and we want to see the rise and the fall of civilisations. Here you can see it precisely, really in the act. But it is not good to be looking into the globe all the time. One needs a change, recreation; recreation means re-creation, it means that cells which enable you to see have got strained by receiving so many pictures very much the same, so you want to turn your eyes away and look at something different. You need a change and that is called re-creation or recreation. Come on into this room." I rose reluctantly to my feet and followed him, dragging my feet with an exaggerated impression of weariness. But the Lama Mingyar Dondup knew all those tricks, he had probably done the same thing to his Guide.

When I reached the door I nearly turned and bolted. There were a lot of people there, men and women. Some of them were naked, and I saw a woman right in front of me, the first naked woman I had every seen and I turned to flee after apologising to the lady for violating her privacy. But the Lama Mingyar Dondup put his hands on my shoulders, and he was laughing so much that he could hardly speak. "Lobsang, Lobsang! The look on your face was worth all the hardships we have had on this trip. These people are preserved people, they once lived on different planets. They were brought here—alive—to act as specimens. They are still quite alive, you know!"

"But, Master, how can they possibly be alive after a million or two years? Why haven't they crumbled into dust?"

"Well, it's again suspended animation. They are in an invisible cocoon which prevents any of the cells from working. But, you know, you will have to come and examine these figures, men and women, because you are going to have a lot to do with women. You are going to study medicine in Chungking, and later you will have an enormous number of women as your patients. So you'd better get to know them now. Here, for instance, is a woman who was almost ready to give birth to a child, and we might revive her and let the child be born for your edification because what we are doing is of greater importance, and if we have to sacrifice one or two or three people then that is worthwhile if it can save this world with its millions of people."

I looked at the people again and felt myself blushing furiously at the sight of the naked women. "Master, there is a woman over there who is completely black, but how can that be? How can one have an entirely black woman?"

"Well, Lobsang, I must say I am astonished at your amazement over this matter. There are people of many different colours, white, tan, brown, and black, and on some worlds there are blue people and green people. It all depends on what sort of food they and their parents and their grandparents were accustomed to eat. It all depends on a secretion in the body which causes the colouration. But you come and examine these people!"

The Lama turned and left me, and went into an inner room. I was left with these people who were not dead yet not alive either. Tentatively I touched the arm of the best looking woman there, and it was not ice cold, it was reasonably warm, much about my own temperature except that my temperature had risen considerably over the last few minutes!

A thought occurred to me. "Master, Master, I have an urgent question."

"Ah, Lobsang, I see that you have picked the most beautiful woman in the whole bunch. Well, let me admire your taste. This is a very fine woman, and we wanted the best because some of the old frumps in some museums absolutely repel one. So the people who planned for this collection picked only the best. But what's your question?" He sat down on a low stool, so I did the same.

I said, "How do people grow, how do they grow to resemble their parents? Why don't they come out as a baby and then resemble a horse or any other creature?"

"People are made up of cells. The controlling cells of the body at a very early age are, what I will term, imprinted with the character and general appearance of the parents. So those cells have an absolute memory of what they should look like, but as one gets older each cell forgets just a bit of what the pattern should be. The cells, we will say, "wander" from the original built-in cell-memory. You may, for instance, have a woman, as you are observing, and she may have been—well—unawakened so that her cells blindly follow the pattern of the cell before. I am telling you all this in the simplest way I can, you will learn more about it at Chakpori, and later at Chungking. But every cell in the body has a definite memory of what it should be like in health. As the body gets older the memory of the original pattern becomes—well—lost or unable, for some reason, to follow the precise pattern, so it diverges slightly from the original cells and then, once having departed from the original pattern, it is easier and easier to forget more and more what the body should look like. We call that aging, and when a body can no longer follow the exact pattern imprinted into the cells then we say that things have deteriorated and the body is mentally sick. After a few more years the change becomes more and more marked, and eventually the person dies."

"But how about people with cancer, how do they manage to get into such a condition?" I asked.

My Guide replied, "We have talked about cells forgetting what pattern they should follow. They forget the pattern which should have been imprinted while the baby was being formed, but we say that when a person has cancer of one type then the memory cells become distorted memory cells, and they order fresh growth to occur where there should be no growth. The result of that is, we get in the human body a large mass which interferes with other organs, perhaps pushing them out of place, and perhaps destroying them. But there are different types of cancer. Another type is that in which the cells that should be controlling growth forget that they are meant to produce fresh cells of a certain type and one gets a complete reversal. Certain organs of the body waste away. The cell is worked out, it has done its share of work, of maintaining the body, and now it needs replacing so the body can continue to exist. But the cell has lost the pattern, forgotten the pattern of growth, if you prefer it in that way, and having forgotten it makes a guess and it either builds fresh cells at a frantic rate or it builds cells which devour healthy cells and leave a bleeding, putrid mass inside the body. Then the body soon dies."

"But, sir," I said, "how can the body know if it is going to be male or female because before the body is born who looks after the formation of the baby."

"Well, that depends on the parents. If you get a growth starting which is alkaline then you get one sex; if you get an acid type of cell then you get the opposite sex, and there are on occasion monsters born. The parents were not really compatible, and what the woman produces is neither male nor female, it may be both, it may even have two heads and perhaps three arms. Well, we know that Buddhists should not take life, but what can be done, how can one let a monster survive? A monster with hardly a rudimentary brain—well, if we let a monster like that grow and propagate their species soon we should have more and more monsters because it seems to us that the bad things multiply more quickly than the good things.

"You will get used to all this when you get to Chungking. I am giving you a rudimentary explanation now so that you know something of what to expect. Now, in a later time I will take you into another room and show you monsters which have been born, and I will show you normal and abnormal cells. And then you will see what a marvellous thing a human body is. But, first of all, examine some of these people especially the women. Here is the book showing what a woman is like outside, and inside. If the person is going to be an attractive woman then her memory cells, that is, the cells which carry the memory to reproduce precisely the body cells just as before, are in good order. Then we have to be sure that the mother has sufficient food of the right type and she has no shocks, etc., etc. And. of course, it usually is not wise to have intercourse when a woman is eight, or so, months pregnant. It may upset the whole balance of things.

"Now, I have to write up the record to say what we were doing here, how we got in, and I have to make a guess at how we are going to get out!"

"But, Master," I said in some exasperation, "what is the point of writing about this when no one ever comes here?"

"Oh, but people do come here, Lobsang, they do come here. The ignorant call their craft U.F.O.'s. They come here and they stay in rooms above this one. They just come to receive messages and tell of what they have discovered. You see, these people are the Gardeners of the Earth. They have a vast store of knowledge, but somehow through the centuries they have deteriorated. First of all these were absolutely god-like people with almost unlimited power. They could do anything, just about anything at all. But then the "Head Gardener" sent some of them down to the Earth which had been formed—I have told you all this before—and then the Gardeners travelling at many times the speed of light went back to their base in another Universe.

"As is so often the case on the Earth, and, indeed, on many other worlds, there was a revolution. Some people did not like the thought of these sages, the Gardeners of the Earth, taking women around with them, especially when the woman was some other man's wife. Inevitably there were quarrels, and the Gardeners split into two parties, what I would call the right party and the break-aways. The break-aways thought that, in view of the long distances they travelled and the hard tasks they did, they were entitled to sexual recreation. Well, when they could not get women of their own race to go with them they came to Earth and picked out the biggest women they could find. Events were not at all pleasant because the men were physically too big for the women, and the party that had come to this Earth quarrelled and broke up into two parties. One went to live in the East, and the other party went to live in the West, and with their great knowledge they built nuclear weapons on the principle of a neutron explosive and a laser weapon. Then they carried out raids on each other's territory, always with the intention of stealing, perhaps kidnapping would sound better, their opponents' women.

"Raids called for counter-raids, and their great ships sped ceaselessly across the world and back again. And what happened is just a matter of history; the smaller party who were the right ones, in desperation dropped a bomb over where the wrong party were living. Nowadays people relate that area to the 'Bible Lands'. Everything was destroyed. The desert, which is now there, was once a sparkling sea with many boats upon its surface. But when the bomb dropped the land tipped and all the water ran away down the Mediterranean and out to the Atlantic, and all the water left in the area was the Nile. We can actually see all this, Lobsang, because we have machines here which will pick up scenes from the past."

"Scenes from the past, Master? Seeing what happened a million years ago? It doesn't seem possible."

"Lobsang, everything is vibration or, if you like, if you want to sound more scientific, you will say that everything has its own frequency. So if we can find the frequency—and we can—of these events we can actually chase them, we can make our instruments vibrate at a higher frequency and so it will rapidly overtake impulses which were sent off a million years ago. And if then we reduce the frequency of our machines then, if we match our frequency with those originally emitted by the sages of old, we can see exactly what happened. It is too early to tell you about all this, but we travel in the fourth dimension so that we can overtake a thing in the third dimension, and then if we just sit still we can actually watch everything that happened, and we can have a good laugh at some of the things written in history books and compare those works of fiction with what really happened. History books are a crime because history distorts what happened, it leads one into wrong ways. Oh yes, Lobsang, we have the machine here, actually in the next room, and we can see what people called the Flood. We can see what people called Atlantis. But, as I told you, Atlantis was just the term for lands which sank. They sank to a certain extent in the area of Turkey, and a certain continent near Japan sank as well. Come in with me, I am going to show you something." The Lama rose to his feet, and I rose and followed him.

"Of course, we have recorded many of these scenes because it is a lot of hard work actually tuning-in to the incidents themselves. But we have tuned very accurately and we have an absolute record of precisely what did occur. Now," he fiddled with some little reels which were in serried ranks against a wall, and at last he stopped at one and continued, "this will do, now take a look at this." He put the little reel in a machine, and the great model of the Earth—oh, it must have been about twenty-five feet in diameter—seemed to come to life again. To my amazement it spun and moved sideways and then moved back a bit further, and it stopped.

I looked at the scene on this world, and then I "looked" no longer. I was there. I had every impression that I was there. There was a beautiful land, the grass was the greenest I had ever seen, and I was standing on the edge of a beach of silver sand. People were there lounging, some had highly decorative and highly suggestive swimsuits, and some wore nothing. They, the ones who wore nothing, certainly looked far more decent than those who had a piece of cloth which merely titillated one's sexual interest.

I looked out across the sparkling sea. The sea was blue, the blue of the sky, and it was a calm day. Little ships with sails were engaged in friendly rivalry, seeing which of them was the fastest, seeing which of them was the best handled. And then—then—all of a sudden, there was a tremendous boom, and the land tipped. Where we were standing the land tipped, and the sea rushed away until before us all we could see was what had been the bottom of the sea.

Scarcely had we drawn breath when a most peculiar sensation affected us. We found that we were rising rapidly up into the air, not just us but the land as well, and the little ridge of rocky hills rose and rose and rose, and it became stupendous mountains, a range of mountains extending as far as the eye could see in any direction.

I seemed to be standing on the very edge of a piece of firm land, and as I cautiously and fearfully peered down I felt sick to my stomach; the land was so high that I thought we must have travelled up to the Heavenly Fields. Not another soul was in sight, I was there alone, frightened, sick at heart. Tibet had risen thirty thousand feet in about thirty seconds. I found that I was panting. The air was rarefied here, and every breath was a gasping effort.

Suddenly, from a split in the mountain range, there sprang a shaft of water under, it seemed, very high pressure. It settled down a bit, and then made its own course down from that high mountain range, right down across the new land which had been the sea bottom. And so was born the mighty Brahmaputra which now has its exit in the Bay of Bengal. But it was not a nice, clean water which reached the Bay of Bengal, it was water polluted with corpses, human, animal, trees, everything. But the water was not the main thing because, to my horrified astonishment, I was rising up, the land was rising up, the mountain was getting higher and higher, and I was going up with it. Soon I was standing in a barren valley ringed with mighty mountains, and we were about thirty thousand feet in the air.

This globe thing, this simulacrum of the world was an absolutely fantastic thing because one was not just looking at the events, one was living the events, actually living them. When I looked at the globe first I thought, "Hmm, some sort of scruffy show like a magic lantern thing, like some of the missionaries bring." But when I looked into the thing I seemed to fall, I seemed to fall out of the clouds, out of the sky, and down, down, to come to rest as lightly as a falling leaf. And then I lived the actual events of millions of years before. This was a product of a mighty civilisation, far, far, beyond the skill of the present day artesans or scientists. I cannot impress upon you sufficiently that this was living it. I found I could walk. For instance, there was a dark shadow which interested me greatly, and I walked toward it, I felt that I actually WAS walking. And then, perhaps for the first time, human eyes looked at the small mountain upon which, in hundreds of centuries to come, the mighty Potala would be built.

"I really cannot understand any of this, Master," I said. "You are trying me beyond the capacity of my brains."

"Nonsense, Lobsang, nonsense. You and I have been together in many, many lives. We have been friends for life after life, and you are going to carry on after me. I have lived four hundred years and more already of this life, and I am the one, the only one in the whole of Tibet, who understands all the workings of these things. That was one of my tasks. And my other task," he looked at me whimsically, "was training you, giving you my knowledge so that when I pass on in the near future with a dagger through my back you will be able to remember this place, remember how to get in, how to use all the appliances, and live again the events of the past. You will be able to see where the world has gone wrong, and I think it is going to be too late in this particular cycle's life to do much about it. But never mind, people are learning the hard way because they reject the easy way. There is no need for all this suffering, you know, Lobsang. There is no need for all this fighting among the Afridi and the British Indian Army, they are always fighting and they seem to think that to fight is the only way to do things. The best way to do a thing is persuasion, not this killing, this raping and murdering and torturing. It hurts the victim, but it hurts the perpetrator more because all this goes back to the Overself. You and I Lobsang, have got a fairly clean record. Our Overself is quite pleased with us."

"You said 'Overself', Master. Does that mean that you and I have the same Overself?"

"Yes indeed it does, young sage, that's just what it does mean. It means that you and I will come together life after life, not merely on this world, not merely in this Universe, but everywhere, anywhere, at any time. You, my poor friend, are going to have a very hard life this time. You are going to be the victim of calumny, there is going to be all manner of lying attacks on you. And yet if people would listen to you Tibet could be saved. Instead of that, in years to come Tibet will be taken over by the Chinese and ruined." He turned away quickly, but not before I saw the tears in his eyes. So I moved away into the kitchen and got a drink of water.

"Master," I said, "I wish you would explain to me how these things do not go bad."

"Well, look at the water you are drinking now. How old is the water? It may be as old as the world itself. It doesn't go bad, does it? Things only go bad when they are treated incorrectly. For instance, supposing you cut a finger and it starts to heal, and you cut it again and it starts to heal, and you cut it again and once more it starts to heal, but not necessarily in the same pattern as it was before you cut it. The cells of regeneration have been confused, they started to grow according to their inbuilt pattern, and then they got cut again. They started once more to grow according to their inbuilt pattern, and so on and so on. And eventually the cells forgot the pattern they should form and instead they grew out in a great lump, and that's what cancer is. Cancer is the uncontrolled growth of cells where they should not be, and if one was taught properly and one had full control of the body there wouldn't be any cancer. If one saw that the cells were what I will call misgrowing then the body could stop it in time. We have preached about this, and preached about it in different countries, and people have absolutely hooted with laughter at these natives daring to come from some unknown country, 'gooks' they call us, gooks, the most worthless things in existence. But, you know, we may be gooks, but in time it will be a word of honour, of respect. If people would listen to us we could cure cancer, we could cure T.B. You had T.B., Lobsang, remember that, and I cured you with your cooperation, and if I hadn't had your cooperation I could not have cured you."

We fell silent in a state of spiritual communion with each other. Ours was a purely spiritual association, without any carnal connotation at all. Of course there were some lamas who used their chelas for wrong purposes, lamas who should not have been lamas but who should have been—well, labourers, anything, because they needed women. We did not need women, nor did we need any homosexual association. Ours, as I said, was purely spiritual like the mingling of two souls who mingle to embrace in the spirit and then withdraw from the spirit of the other feeling refreshed and in possession of fresh knowledge.

There is such a feeling in the world today that sex is the only thing that matters, selfish sex, not for the continuation of the race but just because it gives pleasant sensations. The real sex is that which we have when we leave this world, the communion of two souls, and when we return back to the Overself we shall experience the greatest thrill, the greatest exhilaration of all. And then we shall realise that the hardships we endured on this beastly Earth were merely to drive out impurities from us, to drive out wrong thoughts from us, and in my opinion, the world is too hard. It is so hard, and humans have degenerated so much that they cannot take the hardship, they cannot profit by the hardship, but instead they become worse and worse, and more and more evil, venting their spite on little animals. That is a great pity because cats, for example, are known as the eyes of the Gods. Cats can go anywhere, nobody takes any notice when a cat is sitting there, forelegs folded and tail curled neatly around the body, and eyes half shut—people think the cat is resting. But no, the cat is working, the cat is transmitting all that is happening. Your brain cannot see anything without your eyes. Your brain cannot make a sound without your voice, and cats are another extension of the senses which let the Gardeners of the Earth know what is going on. In time we shall welcome this, in time we shall realise that cats have saved us from many a fatal mistake. It is a pity we don't treat them more kindly, isn't it?

CHAPTER SEVEN

"Lobsang! LOBSANG! Come on, we have some work to do."

I jumped up in such a hurry that I kicked away my shoes, well, sandals; there was no such thing as shoes in Tibet. Everyone wore sandals or, if one was riding a long way, boots which came up to the knees. Anyway, there were my sandals skittering across the floor, and I was skittering across the floor in the opposite direction. I reached the Lama and he said, "Now, we've got to do a bit of history, true history, not the muck they put out in books where things have to be altered so they shall not annoy any man in a powerful position." He led me into what we had come to call the "World Room", and we sat down at the little corner which we called the "console".

It really was a marvellous thing; this simulacrum of the world looked larger than the room which contained it, which everyone would know is impossible. But the Lama divined my thoughts, and he said, "Of course, when we come in here we come under the influence of the fourth dimension, and in the fourth dimension one can have a model which is larger than the room that contains it if that room be of the three dimensions. But let's not worry about that, let's worry about this. What we are seeing in this world is the actual happenings of the world in years gone by, something like an echo. You go and make a loud noise in an echo area, and you get the same sound come back to you. Well, that is a very brief idea of what this is, it's not strictly accurate, of course, because I am trying to tell you in the three dimensions what there is in the fourth and fifth. So you will have to trust your senses as to what you see, and what you see will actually be quite correct." He turned around again, and then said, "We have seen the formation of the world, we have seen the very first creatures—hominides—to be placed on this world, so let us start this at the next stage."

The room darkened and I felt myself falling. Instinctively I grabbed the Lama's arm, and he put an arm around my shoulders. "It's all right, Lobsang, you are not really falling, its just that your brain is changing to accept four dimensions."

Now the falling sensation stopped, and I found myself standing in a shockingly frightening world. There were huge animals there of an ugliness unsurpassed by anything I had seen before. Great creatures went by, flapping through the air with the most hideous sound, it sounded like old unoiled leather. Wings which could barely support the body of the creature. But these flew around and occasionally one went down to the ground to pick up a piece of food which had fallen from some other flying creature. But once down, they stayed down, their wings were insufficient to get them in the air again, and they had no legs with which to help themselves.

Indescribable noises came from the marsh to my left, they were shocking noises, and I felt sick with fright. And then, quite close to me, out of the muck of the marsh, there emerged a tiny head on top of a vast neck. The neck must have been about twenty feet long, and there were many underwater struggles before the thing dragged itself ashore. It had a round body, and then a tail which tapered to balance the contours of the neck and the head.

But as I was looking at that thing, and afraid that it might be looking at me, I heard horrid crashes and cracks as if some vast thing was charging through the forest and snapping off tree trunks like we would snap

111

a straw. I caught a glimpse of the largest creature I had ever seen.

The Lama said, "Let's go on a century or two and find when the humans first came."

I seemed to doze or something because when I looked at the globe again—no, no—of course not, I was ON the globe, I was IN the globe, part of it. But, anyway, when I looked up again I saw some horrid looking creatures marching along, there were six of them, and they were beetle-browed with hardly any neck, and they each carried a great chunk of tree as a weapon, tapering to a handgrip at one end and the other end having a nice knot or burl which would be stronger than the ordinary wood of which the trunk was composed. These creatures marched along, One, a woman, was feeding a baby at her breast as she marched, and they made not a sound although they were going along marshy ground, there was no squelching or splashing, just complete silence. I watched them go out of sight, and then, once again, I seemed to have a doze because when I looked up again I saw a marvellous city. The city was made of shining stones of different colours, there were bridges across the streets, and there were mechanical birds which flew along the streets with people in them. These things could stop and hover in the air while people got in or got out. Then, all of a sudden, everyone turned and gazed toward the distant skyline, over the mountain range. From there there came a vast roaring, and soon a whole flock of these mechanical birds came along and they circled over the city. People were running everywhere. Some were on their knees praying, but the priests, I noted, did not stop to pray, they put all their energy into running. After some minutes of this circling doors opened in the bottom of these mechanical things, and metal boxes fell out. The mechanical birds closed the doors in their undersides, and they sped off. The city rose up into the air, and fell to the ground as dust, and then we heard the bang and the concussion because sight is so much quicker than hearing. We heard the screams of the people, people trapped beneath beams or buried in dust. Again, there came a doze, this is all I can call it—a doze—because I was unaware of any break between what I had been seeing and what I was seeing now. It was a later age, and I could see a city being built, a grand city, one of surpassing beauty. It was real artistry. Spires soared high into the sky, and there were delicate traceries of metal joining one building to another. There were people about, people going about their everyday business, shopping, selling, standing on street corners and discussing things. Then there came a roaring, a terrific roaring, and an immense flock of these mechanical birds passed overhead in formation, and all the people laughed, cheered and waved. The mechanical birds proceeded upon their way undisturbed. They crossed the mountain range, and then we heard terrible bangs and crashes, and we knew that "our side" were paying back the enemy for the destruction that they had caused. But—but mechanical birds were returning, or not returning, because they were not ours, they were different, some were of different shapes, many were of different colours, and they came over our city and they dropped their bombs again. Our city was swept by a fire storm, the fire roared and raged, and everything in the city burned and fell to the ground. Delicate traceries of bridges turned red and then white, and then they melted, and the liquid metal fell like rain. Soon I was standing on a plain, the only thing there. There were no trees, the artificial lakes had gone, turned into steam, and I stood there and I looked about me, and I wondered what was the sense of it all, why were these Gardeners of the Earth fighting against other Gardeners? I could not make any sense at all out of it.

Then the world itself shook and darkened. I found myself sitting on a chair beside the Lama Mingyar Dondup. He was looking sadder than I had ever seen anyone look before. "Lobsang, this has happened on this world for millions of years. There have been people of a high degree of culture, but somehow they have quarrelled with others, and each side has bombed or shelled the other side so that only a few humans were left, and they hid in caves and in a few years they crept out to start again with a fresh civilisation. And that civilisation in its turn would be destroyed, and all the remnants would be ploughed deep into the soil by the farmers who were trying to grow crops in the battle-torn land."

The Lama looked exceedingly sad, and he sat with his chin cupped in his hands. And then he said, "I could show you the whole history of the world, but it would take the whole of your lifetime to view it. So I will only show you some flashes, as we call it, and I will tell you about others. It is a very sad thing but various types of people have been tried as settlers on this world. There has been an all-black race, it came after a big turmoil. Two white races had been quarrelling as to who was the most powerful, and, of course, they resorted to warfare. It's always warfare, always the evil thoughts of people. If people would only believe in a God there would be none of this trouble. But this all-black race made a horrible mess of things on the world until at last they reached a very high degree of civilisation, far higher than our civilisation now. But then two different races of the black people quarrelled and they sought frantically to get a more powerful weapon than their opponents. Well, they did, and somehow the signal was given to release these—well—rocket things, and that caused tremendous trouble on this world. Most of the people were wiped out, just wiped out like one would kill off a colony of fierce ants.

"Always there are some survivors, and so now we have a white race, a black race, and a yellow race. At one time there was a green race. People in those days lived for hundred of years because their "memory cells" were able to reproduce dying cells with exactitude. It is only since the cells lost their ability to reproduce accurately that we have such short lives. But in one of the wars there were tremendous explosions, and most of the cloud cover of the Earth was blown away, blown away into space, and the sunlight came pouring in with all the lethal rays. And instead of people living seven or eight hundred years their lifespan was just about seventy years.

"The sun isn't the kind, benevolent provider of sunlight, etc., etc. It sends out rays which cause harm to people. You can see for yourself that people exposed to the sunlight too much have their skin turn dark. Now if it was good to have sunlight then Nature would not need to make a shield against the light. But the rays, ultra-violet, and others, affected the humans and made them worse, and the two sets of Gardeners of the Earth became even fiercer. One side was good and wanted to see the human race grow fruitful and do much good; instead of that, people exposed to too much sunlight used to get T.B. or cancer. All the surfaces of the world, or rather, all the surfaces of the people of the world, were prone to diseases, skin diseases of various forms, and they were tenacious, there was no cure for them. After all, these rays could penetrate many feet of stone, and it was useless for the inhabitants of the world to live in houses because the rays could still reach them.

"There is an old saying that there were giants in those days. Yes, that is true. The giants were one set of the Gardeners of the Earth. They stood two or three times the height of the average human, and they were slow moving, somewhat lethargic, and did not like to work. They tried to get back to their home base, but when they tried they found that there had been troubles on the home base. One set of Gardeners were good and with a good leader, but the other side was a bad side. They throve on wickedness of all kinds, and they were immune to the appeals of those who wanted a peaceful world with a more healthy lifespan.

"These good Gardeners saw how useless it was to stay at their home base, so they reprovisioned their ships and put in fresh fuel rods, and they took off again for Earth.

"Their ships could travel faster than light. They could travel so fast that no human could control them, and they had to be worked by a form of computer which had a special shield to keep away meteorites, or other obstructions, otherwise without these shields the ships would have been riddled with meteorites or cosmic dust resulting, of course, in loss of air and the death of all aboard.

"At last they got back to the Earth and they found another war in progress. The wrong side—the bad part of the Gardeners of the Earth—had mixed too freely with the Earth people, and taught them many of their secrets. Since those days the world has been getting worse and worse, and there will have to be a fresh world war during which many people will die. Many more will go into hiding in caves or in high mountain clefts. They were told by their Sages of all that was going to happen, so they took the view that what was the good of living a good life when, in a few short years, perhaps the Earth itself would be destroyed. And we are getting perilously close to that time now."

I listened to all this, and then I said, "I have been told by the head astrologer that I am going to have an awful life, a really sick life. Now, how is that going to help the world?"

The Lama said, "Yes, everything the head astrologer said has come to pass, and it is true that you are going to have a very, very bad time with everyone's hand against you. But always remember that you will succeed in what you are doing, and when you leave this world you will not be stuck in the astral, you will go to a much higher station. And, of course, you will never return to the Earth. I am not sure if it's time yet to tell you of all the things that are going to happen here, but let us have a look at some of the events of the past. I think, though, that first we should have a meal because these three dimension pictorial realisations tire one and one forgets the time."

We were true to our native food, tsampa, and cold water to drink. But then the Lama said, "You will have to get used to different food because in other parts of the world they do not know anything at all about tsampa, they have food which is precooked, sealed in

116

a can, and as long as the can is kept intact the food is edible no matter how long it is kept before eating. But, of course, one also has to keep the cans at a cold temperature, that stops the decay. Nowadays in the West they use what they call ice boxes, great big boxes packed with ice which surrounds the cans of food, and every few days the boxes have to be opened to see how much of the ice has melted. If a lot has melted then the whole box has to be repacked with fresh ice. You can always tell, though, when the food has gone bad because the cans will bulge showing that there is a gas pressure, the gas of decomposition inside. And then one has to throw away such cans or get poisoned.

"Now let us clean our bowls, and then we will look once again at this world of which we are part." The Lama rose to his feet and scraped away the remnants of tsampa, and then he went to a little pile of sand, took a handful, and cleaned his bowl with it. I followed suit, and I thought what an awful chore it was having to clean dishes every time. I wondered why no one had invented something to hold food and then be discarded when the food upon it had been eaten. I thought of all the monks and all the lamas busy with their handful of fine sand, but that is a lot more healthy than washing a wooden bowl, you know. If you have a thing wet then, obviously, it is going to seep into the wood. And suppose you have some nice juicy fruit in your bowl; you eat the fruit and there is some juice left, and if you go and wash that bowl then you are saturating the wood and allowing juices to enter. No, until there is a better system very fine sand is much, much better than water.

"How long do you think this world has been a world, sir?"

The lama smiled at me and said, "Well, you have already seen part of it, and I think we ought to see a bit more of the world, past, present and future, don't you?"

We walked slowly towards that great hall or room where the simulacrum of the world lay waiting to be used. "You know, Lobsang, we all tend to think that this world is for ever and for ever, and yet this Universe is actually being destroyed now. It has been established quite definitely that all the worlds are rushing away from each other. Now, really the best way to explain it is to tell you again that the time on this world is entirely artificial. The real time is space time, and do you remember those fusees which I showed you and which could be struck on something rough and the end would explode into flame? Well, if you are a God in space the birth, life and death of this world or any other world would resemble the striking of that fusee. First there is the heat engendered by the friction of the fusee point on something hard. Then the point bursts into flame, and then the flame dies out and you've got just a red hot head to the fusee which quickly cools to become just a black burned mass. Earth is like that, and all the other planets. To us living on this Earth the Earth seems forever, but supposing you had a minute, minute person who could be placed on the head of the fusee as it was cooling, he would think that he was living on a world which would exist for ever and for ever. Do you get what I am driving at?"

"Yes, sir, I do. I was told by a lama who had been to a big school in Germany, and he said that a fusee simile is appropriate. He used almost the same words as you, but he added that after several million years the head of the match, or the world, would reach about twenty million degrees Fahrenheit because it needs a certain temperature before the hydrogen in the atmosphere can be converted to carbon, oxygen and various other elements. All these elements are necessary in the formation of the world. He told me, also, that before the end of the world the world globe swells."

"Yes, that is absolutely true. You have to remember that in the Western world they do not know of these things because they haven't anything like we have here. Here we actually have the instruments which super-scientists of perhaps a billion years ago built— built to last a billion years or more. These machines have stood here throughout the hundreds, throughout the thousands of centuries, until someone came along who knew how to work them. I know how to work them, Lobsang, and I am going to teach you, and you are going to have a life of hardship so that you know what the world is really like. And because of the teaching which you can take back to Patra you can make it easier for other worlds."

"But, sir, you have mentioned the word "Patra", but I know of no world with that name," I said.

"No, I am aware of that, but you will do before long. I am going to show you Patra in this world, but there are so many things to see first, and I have always found it to be useless to have an instrument which would produce predictable results, but then, if the operator did not know how to work the machine and how the final result was arrived at, then he would be a very poor operator indeed. No instrument should be used unless the prospective operator can do the things which the instrument has been designed to do."

We reached the room, it should be called a hall, really, because of the size of it, but we reached the room or hall, or whatever you want to call it, and we entered. Immediately there was a faint glow and we saw dawn beginning to turn to daylight. It was a different sort of dawn than we should see now because now all those glorious colours which we see at sunrise and sunset are merely reflections from the pollution in the atmosphere. In those days the "pollution" was actually food for the Earth, food for the soil being screwed out onto the land from the volcanoes, and it is these volcanoes which gave the seas their salt content. Without salt one could not live.

We sat down by that console thing, and the Lama Mingyar Dondup said, "Let us look at some random spots. We've got all the time we need, they will probably be glad to get us out of their way, especially you, you young wretch, dropping things on peoples' bald heads. But in the early days animals, the first form of life on Earth, were weird creatures indeed. For instance, the brachiosaurus was probably the strangest creature that has ever been seen on this Earth. There are all manner of strange things. For example, ultrasaurus was a most peculiar animal. It would have a very high blood pressure because its head could be more than sixty feet in the air, and furthermore that animal weighed about eighty tons, and it had two brains, the one in the head moved the jaws and the front legs, and the one at its behind, that is, right behind the pelvis, is there to work the tail and rear legs. It always reminds me of a question I was asked, 'What happens if a centipede gets its legs out of step?' Well, that is a question I could not answer with any degree of accuracy. I could only say that perhaps the creature had some special other creature watching over it to see that it didn't go cross-legged."

"Well, Lobsang, what shall we look at? We have ample time and so you tell me what you want to see most."

I thought for a time, and then I said, "That Japanese lama we had, he told us a lot of peculiar things, I still don't know whether to believe him or not. He told us that the world was once very hot, and then all of a sudden it became very cold and the surface of the world was covered with ice. Can we see that?"

"Yes, of course we can. There is no difficulty at all. But, you know, this has happened several times. You see, the world is billions of years old and every so many millions of years there is an ice age. For instance, at the North Pole now there is a depth of ice in the water of six hundred feet, and if all the ice melted and the icebergs also melted everyone on Earth would be drowned because the land would be inundated—well, except for we of Tibet, and we would be too high for the water to reach." He turned to the console and looked up a whole column of figures, and then the light in the big hall, or room, or whatever you want to call it, dimmed. For seconds we were in darkness and then there came a reddish glow, most peculiar, absolutely peculiar, and from the poles, the North and the South Poles, there came variegated streaks of light.

"That is the aurora borealis, or aura of the world. We can see it because, although we appear to be on Earth, we are away from that manifestation, that is why we see it." The light grew brighter, it grew dazzlingly bright, so bright that we had to view it through almost closed eyes.

"Where is Tibet?" I asked.

"We are standing on it, Lobsang, we are standing on it. All that that you are looking at down there is ice."

I was looking at that ice wondering what it could be because—well, there was green ice, there was blue ice, and there was absolutely transparent ice, as transparent as the clearest of clear water. I just could not make it out, so I said, "I've seen enough of that, that is a dismal sight." The Lama laughed and turned back to the things on the console, and the world turned and flickered with speed. Then it was turning so fast that everything was grey, there was no darkness and no lightness, only this grey impression, and then the world slowed down and we found that we were looking at a great city, a fantastic city. It was a city built just before the advent of the Sumerians. It was built by a race of whose existence there is now no written trace, nothing in history about it and, in fact, there was only the remotest mention of Sumerians in the history books. But they came as conquerors and they looted, raped, and ravished the city, and having reduced it to a state when no stone stood upon another stone they moved on and—according to the history books—they moved out somewhere and no trace has ever been found. No, of course not, because they moved away and they moved off the Earth in huge space ships. I could not understand why these people should be so savage as to come and just destroy a city—well, apparently for the fun of it. Of course they took a lot of women prisoners and that might have been some of the reason.

It occurred to me that I was looking at something which could change the whole history of mankind. "Master," I said, "I have been looking at all these things, looking at all these wonderful, wonderful inventions, but it seems that only a very few people know about them. Now, surely, if everyone knew about them we could have a time when there would be peace throughout the world because what would there be to fight about if everything could be known through these instruments or machines?"

"No, Lobsang, it is not so, old man, it's not so. If there was any thought that people would know about this then crooked financiers would rush in with their armed guards and they would seize all this and kill all of us who know about it, and then they would use the instruments to control the world. Think of it. A crooked capitalist being the king of the world, and everyone else would be his slave."

"Well, I can't understand the attitude of people because we know Tibet is going to be invaded by the Chinese, we know they are going to take all our treasured books away to study. What's to prevent them from capturing the world?"

"Lobsang, my dear friend, you must be very, very simple, weak in the head or something. You don't think we would let any conqueror get hold of things like this, do you? To start with, we have absolute duplicates of these right up in the high Arctic where men can hardly manage to move because of the cold. But inside the mountain ranges there everything is warm and peaceful and comfortable, and we would have eyes on the world, we could see just what was happening, and if necessary we could take some action. But this stuff here—" he gestured around, "all this will be wrecked, blown up, and even booby trapped. First the British and the Russians will try to capture Tibet, but they will fail, they will cause a terrible amount of deaths, but they will fail to conquer. But they will give the Chinese the idea of how to succeed, and the Chinese will come and they will conquer Tibet, conquer part of it, that is. But still they will not get any of these machines, they will not get any of the Holy books or the medical books because we have known of this for years, for centuries, actually, and false books have been prepared and they are ready to be put in place as soon as the Chinese start to invade. The Prophecy, you know, says that Tibet will survive until wheels come to our country, and when wheels come to Tibet that will be the end of our country. So have no fear, all our treasures, all our great sciences from a few million years ago, are safely hidden. I know the location, I have been there. And you, too, are going to know the location because you are going to be shown. I shall be killed in your lifetime, in fact before you leave Tibet, and you will be one of the very, very few who can work these machines and who know how to service them."

"Good gracious, sir, to learn to service these machines would take several lifetimes."

"No, you will learn that they are self-repairing. You have to do just a few manipulations and the machine, or rather, other machines, will repair the faulty machine. You see, they won't have much longer to live, these machines, because starting in several years time, 1985, circumstances will change and there will be a third World War which will last for quite a time, and after the year 2000 there will be many, many changes, some for the better, some for the worse. We are able to see through the Akashic Record of Probabilities. Now, Man is not on rails, you know, unable to deviate from a certain path. Man has free choice within certain limits, those limits being set by the astrological type of the person. But we can very accurately see what happens to a country, and that is what we shall soon be doing because I want you to see some of the wonders of the world. We will tune-in to different situations, to different times."

"But, sir, how is it possible for you to tune-in to sounds which have long passed by, sounds, pictures, and all that? When a thing has happened it is done and finished with."

"Not so, Lobsang, not so. Matter is indestructible, and the impressions of what we say or do go out from us and circle the Universe, and circle the Universe again and again. With this big machine we can go back to about two billion years. Mind, at two billion years the picture is a bit hazy but still bright enough for us to make out what it is."

"Well, I can't understand," I said, "how one can pick up pictures and sounds out of nothingness."

"Lobsang, in a few years to come there will be something called wireless. It is being invented now, and with it one can pick up what will be called radio programmes, and if the receiver is good enough you can pick up from any transmitter in the world, and later still they will have these radio boxes which can pick up pictures. It has all been done before, but as civilisations succeed civilisation sometimes the same things are re-invented. Sometimes an improved version results, but in this case, apparently, the thing called wireless is giving a lot of trouble because the information has to be brought from the astral world by scientists who think they invented it. But, anyway, you just take my word for it that we can go on and see what is going to happen in the world. Unfortunately our upper limit will be three thousand years, beyond that—no—we cannot reach, our pictures are too hazy, too muzzy, for us to decipher them. But you are going to have a lot of suffering and a lot of travelling, and you are going to be the victim of various unscrupulous people who will not like what you are doing and so they will try to blacken your character. On this machine within the next few days you are going to see quite a lot of the highlights of your career. But let us just look at some odds by tuning-in to things at random. Now, look, here is the important happenings in a place called Egypt." The Lama adjusted various controls, and we saw darkness, and up on the skyline of the darkness there were some black triangles. It didn't make sense to me at all, so he gradually advanced one control and the world gradually came into daylight. He said, "Look, this is the building of the Pyramids. People will wonder and wonder in later years however these great blocks of stone were moved around without all sorts of machinery. They are moved by levitation."

"Yes, sir," I replied, "I have heard a lot about levitation, but I haven't the faintest idea how it works."

"Well, you see, the world has a magnetic pull. If you throw a thing up into the air the magnetism of the Earth pulls it down again. If you fall out of a tree you fall down, not up, because the magnetism of the Earth is such that you must fall to the Earth. But we have a thing which is anti-magnetic to the Earth, we have to keep them very carefully under guard the whole time because if an untrained person got hold of one of these things he could find that he had floated right out of the Earth. The fall then is upwards. How we control it is by having two grids, one is tuned to the magnetism of the Earth, the other is opposed to the magnetism of the Earth. Now, when the grids are in a certain position the plates will float, they will not go up and they will not go down. But if you push a lever which alters the relationship of the grids to each other, then in one direction the lever makes the Earth magnetism the stronger, and so the plates, or machine, sink down to the Earth. But if we want to rise up then we push the lever the other way so that the anti-magnetism takes effect and the Earth repels instead of attracts, and so we can rise up into the air. It is the thing the Gods used when they were making this world as it is now. One man could lift up these hundred ton blocks and put them in position without exerting himself, and then, when the block was in the precise position desired, the magnetic current would be switched off and the block would be locked in position by the pull of gravity of the Earth. That is how the Pyramids were built, that is how many strange things, unaccountable things, were built. For example, we have had maps of the Earth for centuries, and we are the only people who have these maps because we alone have these anti-gravity devices and they have been used to map the world exactly. But this is no time to be discussing things. I think we should have a meal, and then we will look at my legs, and after that let us go to sleep for there is a brand new day tomorrow, a day you have never seen before."

CHAPTER EIGHT

"Lobsang! Come on, it's lesson time." My mind went back to another lesson time. It was at the Potala. I had been away a few days with the Lama Mingyar Dondup, and then when we returned to the Potala he said, "Well, lessons will just have started for this afternoon, you'd better go in to the class now." I nodded somewhat despondently and walked in to the classroom. The Lama Teacher looked up and then an expression of rage came to his face, he pointed his finger at me and shouted, "Out! Out! I won't have you in my class."

So there was nothing else for it, I turned around and walked out. Some of the other chelas tittered a bit, and the Lama Teacher descended upon them with his cane flailing everywhere.

I went out into what we called our playground and idly scuffed at the earth. The Lama Mingyar Dondup turned a corner and saw me, and he came across to me and said, "I thought you had gone to class."

"I did, sir," I replied, "but the Teacher was in a rage with me and he ordered me out and said that there would be no more room in his classes for me."

"Oh did he?" said my Guide. "Come along, we will go and see what it's all about together."

We walked side by side along the corridor. The corridor floor was quite slippery with melted butter which had dripped from our butter oil lamps, and the melted butter had fallen to the floor and hardened with the

127

cold and the wretched place was sometimes like a skating rink. But we walked along together to the classroom, and we entered. The Lama Teacher was in a furious rage, lashing out at boys at random. When he saw the Lama Mingyar Dondup he turned very pale indeed, it gave him a nasty shock, and he went back to his podium.

"What is the trouble here?" asked the Lama Mingyar Dondup.

"There is no trouble here except that that boy" (pointing at me) "always disturbs the class. We don't know if he is going to be in the class or out of the class, and I am not having a boy like that to teach."

"Oh, so it's like that, eh? This boy, Lobsang Rampa, is under special orders from the Great Thirteenth, and you will obey those orders just as I do. Come with me, we will go and see the Great Thirteenth now." The Lama Mingyar Dondup turned and walked out of the room with the Lama Teacher following him meekly, still clutching his stick.

"My!" said a boy, "I wonder what's going to happen now, I thought he was going mad. He lashed out at all of us and you can see we've got bruised marks on our faces. I wonder what's going to happen now."

He hadn't long to wait because quite soon the Lama Mingyar Dondup appeared and in his wake there followed a fairly young, studious-looking Lama. The Lama Mingyar Dondup solemnly introduced him to us, and said, "He will be your Teacher from now on, and I want to see a great improvement in behaviour and in the work you do." He turned to the new Teacher and said, "Lobsang Rampa is under special orders. Sometimes he will be away from this class for days. You will do your best to help him catch up on those missing days."

The two Lamas gravely bowed to each other, and Mingyar Dondup then left.

I could not understand why that memory had come up all of a sudden, but—"Hey, Lobsang, you haven't heard a word I have said, have you?"

"No, sir, I was thinking of that time when I could

128

not be accepted into a class, and I was just wondering how such a Lama could become a Teacher as well."

"Oh well, you get good people and you get bad people, and I suppose this time we got a bad one. But never mind, everything is settled. We could say now that I am your Keeper. I don't know if I have to have a lead or a collar for you, or what, but I am your Keeper, and I say what happens to you and no other Teacher can say." He smiled at me as I broke into a really broad smile. I could learn with Mingyar Dondup. He did not stop at the regulation stuff, but he went on to tell us things about the great outer world which he had travelled so much.

"Well, Lobsang, we'd better start at a fairly elementary stage because you will have to teach people in the great outer world, and although you probably know all the first part which I am going to tell you, yet repetition won't hurt you a bit. It might even drive the knowledge in another inch or two." The way he said it was a compliment, and I resolved anew to be a credit to him. Whether I have succeeded or failed only time will tell, when we get back to Patra.

"We will imagine a living body. The person lies down and goes to sleep, and then his astral form will come out of that body and will travel to some place and if the sleeper is fairly unevolved he will wake up thinking he has had a dream and nothing more. But when we get a trained person that person can apparently be soundly asleep while all the time he is doing controlled astral travel and is still aware of what is happening near his physical body. He will get out of the physical body and travel to wherever he wants to, wherever he has been directed to go. You can travel to anywhere on the world by astral travel, and if you train yourself you can remember every single thing that happened when you return to your flesh body.

"When a person dies it is because the astral person wants to get rid of the flesh body. Perhaps the flesh body is disabled and will not function properly, or perhaps the flesh body has learned everything that he needed to learn in that particular incarnation because people come back to Earth time after time until their lessons are learned. You and I are different because we are from bey ona the astral, we are from Patra with which we will deal a little later.

"When the astral form is completely free from the physical body and the Silver Cord is severed and the Golden Bowl be shattered then the entity who was in that body is free to move about, free to do more or less as he wants to do. And then after a time he gets tired of just—well—running wild, and he consults a special branch of the Government whose sole task it is to advise astral people as to what would be best for them, should they stay in the astral and learn a bit more there, or should they go back to the Earth in different circumstances so that they can learn the hard way. You see, when people are in the Overself stage—oh, that is a long way from you just yet, Lobsang—then they cannot experience pain, and people learn more quickly by pain than they do by kindness. So perhaps it will be mapped out that this person shall go back to Earth with an urge to murder, he will be born to parents who are most likely to give him the opportunity of murdering someone. Now, his task is to fight against his inbuilt desire to murder, and if he gets through life without killing another person then that life will have been a complete success. He is learning to control himself, and in that case he will be able to have a rest in the astral, and then, once again, he will approach the Committee of Advisers to see what next they need him to do. He may be given an inclination to be a great missionary, teaching the wrong things. Well, again, he is born to parents who can give him the opportunity of being a missionary, and then it all depends upon how satisfactory he is in that work, and if he realises that he is teaching the wrong things then he might make a change and gather much benefit from it. He might, for instance, realise that there can't be a virgin birth unless the offspring be female. Under certain circumstances women can produce children without the no doubt pleasurable aid of a man, but on every occasion the child so born will be female. If she grows up and marries and has a child then the child may be female or may be a weak, sickly male. You never get a dominant person born without the aid of a man.

"In the astral people can see their mistakes and perhaps do something to overcome the bad they have done to other people. Did you know, Lobsang, that every person on Earth has had to live through the whole of the Zodiac and all the quadrants of the Zodiac as well because the astrological make-up of a person has a very great bearing on how he progresses and his station in life. For example, an Aries person might come and be a very successful butcher, but if his parents are of high enough status he might become a very successful surgeon, not much difference between them, you know. I am told that a pig and a human taste much the same, not that I have ever tried it or intend to try it."

I thought of this for a moment or two, and then I said, "Master, does this mean that we have to live through each sign of the Zodiac—Mars, Venus, and all the others—and then live through the same astrological Sun sign with all the different quadrants?"

"Well, yes, of course it does. The difference that is made by each quadrant is almost unbelievable, because if we get a strong Sun sign then the first part of the quadrant will contain not only the Sun sign but also strong indications from the sign before. Whereas in the centre of the quadrants the Sun sign will be the predominant influence and then, as one progresses through that sign, as we come to the last part of the quadrant then the indications are very strong for the next sign on the chart. I am telling you all this because you may have to explain things like it to people in the future. So every person lives through every part of the Zodiac. not necessarily in the same order but in that order which enables them to profit the most from the things that have to be learned."

"I keep being reminded, Master, that I am going to have a quite hard life with much suffering, etc., etc. Well, why does there have to be so much suffering?"

The Lama Mingyar Dondup looked down at his feet for a moment or two, and then he said, "You have a very great task to do, a noble task, and you will find that people who are not themselves noble will try to prevent you from having any success, and they will stoop to any sort of trick to prevent you from achieving success. You see, people get jealous, people make something, write something, or draw something which is acknowledged to be far better than a book or drawing which was the undisputed leader before your effort. Now, I know I sound all mixed up on that, but that's just how it is. You will have to count on a terrific amount of jealousy and—you poor soul—you will have a lot of trouble caused by women, not through your sexual activities with them, but someone's wife will show friendship to you and her husband, not understanding, will be insanely jealous. And then other women will be jealous because they smiled at you and you didn't smile back at them. Oh, Lobsang, beware of women, I have all my life and I feel the better for it."

I sat in black gloomy silence thinking over my terrible fate, and then the Lama said, "Cheer up, I know that you know nothing at all about women, but soon you will have an opportunity to examine their bodies inside and outside because when you leave here to go to Chungking in a few years you will see dead bodies, male and female, in the dissecting rooms. At first you will find that your stomach will heave quite a bit, but no matter, a day or two and you will be quite used to it, and from the Record of Probabilities you are going to be a very good doctor indeed. You can be a good surgeon because—well, I must say it—you are a bit ruthless and one has to be ruthless to be a good surgeon. So when we get out of this cell, or cage, or cave, call it what you will, you will soon go to another where you will have a bit of practise with surgical instruments and where you can learn things through the universal language. And, of course, I stand ready to help you in any way possible."

"Master, you have mentioned Patra several times within the last few days, but I have never heard of the word before and I am sure that not too many people in the Potala or Chakpori make much use of the word."

"Well, there is no point in mentioning a thing which is far, far beyond the average person's attainment. Patra is the Heavenly Fields of the Heavenly Fields. All people, when they leave the Earth, go to the astral world. It actually is a world, as you should have seen through your astral travels. It is a world just like this Earth in many ways, but there are many more pleasant facets to it, you can mix with people, you can read, you can talk, and you can go to meetings and hear how others are getting on. Why did this person fail, and why did that person succeed. But from the astral people return to Earth or to some other planet in order to carry out another and more successful life. But there is a rare, rare planet called Patra. It is the Heaven of Heavens, only the very best souls go there, only those who have done most good. For example, Leonardo da Vinci is there working on projects which will help other "earths". Socrates is there. Aristotle and many of that type are there. You won't find any fakes there, that excludes one quite definitely, and it is already planned that you are going to Patra at the end of this life. You are going there because, for several lives, you have had hardship after hardship, and you have successfully surmounted them, and the task you are doing now—well, anyone else would say it was an impossible task, but you will succeed and you will stay on Patra for quite a time. There is no friction there, no fights, no starvation or cruelty."

"Will cats be permitted on Patra, Master?"

"Oh my goodness, yes, of course they will. Cats have souls just the same as people. There are a lot of ignoramuses who think that this thing on four legs is just a dumb animal, almost without feeling and certainly without intelligence, and definitely without a soul. That is not true. Cats have souls, cats can progress. They can progress through the world of the Astral and read about Patra. In Patra they can be with the people they loved on Earth, or perhaps on some other planet. Oh yes, Lobsang, you must make it quite clear to people that cats are people, they are individuals, they are highly evolved little people who have been put on Earth for a special purpose. So you should treat cats with great respect, as I know you do.

"Let's take a walk around because my legs are getting stiff, and I think I am ready for a bit of a walk to try and loosen them up. So come on, stir those lazy legs of yours, and we will walk around and see some other things that you haven't seen before."

"Master!" I called out to the Lama Mingyar Dondup who was quite a way ahead of me now. He stopped to permit me to catch up with him, and then I went on, "Master, you know this place well, you know it very well, and I thought it was a discovery. You've been teasing me, Master."

He laughed and said, "No, I haven't been teasing you, Lobsang, and the particular entrance we came in—well that was a surprise. I certainly did not expect an entrance there because there is nothing about it on the maps, and I am rather wondering why there should have been an entrance there. You agree with me that there was no sign of a rock deformation. I suppose it must have been because that old hermit was in charge of various supplies here and he liked to have this entrance so close to his hermitage. But—no, no, I wasn't teasing you. We shall have to find out how to get out tomorrow because now my legs have healed so well I can manage to climb down the mountain."

I replied, "Well, you won't look very pretty climbing down the mountain with your robes in such tatters."

"Ah yes I will. You and I are going to appear tomorrow in brand new robes which are about a million years old!" Then, as an afterthought, "And you are going to appear as a monk, not as a chela or acolyte. From now on you have to stay with me and go where I go, and learn anything that I can tell you." He turned away, walked just a few steps, bowed to a door, and placed his hands in a certain position. Slowly I saw a section of the wall slide aside in utter silence, no grating of rock upon rock, utter silence, such silence as to make the whole thing uncanny.

The Lama gave me a little push between the shoulder blades, and said, "Come on, this is some stuff you have to see. This is Patra. This is how Patra would appear to us. Of course this globe," and he gestured to a great globe which absolutely filled a large hall, "is merely so that we can see what is going on in Patra at any time." He put his hand on my shoulder, and we walked a few yards until we came to a wall fitted with instruments and a great big screen—oh, about four men high and three men wide. He said, "That is for any particular detail investigation."

The lights in the hall dimmed. Similarly, at the same rate, the light from the globe which he had called Patra brightened. It was a sort of—well—pinkish-gold colour, and it gave one a wonderful feeling of warmness and the sensation that one was truly welcome.

The Lama pushed one of those button things again and the haziness in the globe, or around the globe, disappeared like a mountain fog disappearing before the rays of the sun. I peered avidly. This was a wonderful world indeed. I seemed to be standing on a stone wall, and waves were beating mildly against the wall. Then, just to my right, I saw a ship coming in. I knew it was a ship because I had seen pictures of them. But this ship came in and moored up against the wall just in front of me, and a lot of people got off all looking pleased with themselves.

"Well, that's a happy looking crowd, Master. What were they doing, anyway?"

"Oh, this is Patra. Here you can have any number of things for recreation. These people, I suppose, thought how nice it would be to take a leisurely trip over to the island. I expect they had tea there and then they came back.

"This is several steps up from the astral world. People can only come here if they are, let us say, super people. It often entails terrible suffering to get worthy

135

of this place, but when one gets here and sees what it is, and sees the calibre of the people, then it is obvious that the place is worth all the suffering.

"Here we can travel by thought. We are on this planet and we want to see a certain person. Well, we think about him, we think about him hard, and if he is willing to see us we suddenly lift off the ground, and rise up in the air and travel swiftly to our wanted destination. We should get there and we should see the person we wanted to see standing outside his front door ready to greet us."

"But, Master, what sort of people come here, how do they get here? And would you call them prisoners? Presumably they can't get away from this place."

"Oh definitely, definitely this is not a prison. This is a place of advancement, only good people can come here. Those who have made supreme sacrifices, can come, those who have done their very best to help their fellow men and women. Normally we should go from the flesh body to the astral body. Do you see that here no one has a Silver Cord? No one has a Golden Bowl vapour around his or her head? They don't need it here because everyone is the same. We have all manner of good people here. Socrates, Aristotle, Leonardo da Vinci, and others like that. Here they lose what little faults they had because to keep them on Earth they had to adopt a fault. They were of such a high vibration that they just could not stay on Earth without having some sort of fault, so before Mendelsohn, or someone else, could get down to Earth he had to have a fault inbred for that one particular life. So when he died and got to the astral world then the fault departed, and the entity departed also. I mentioned Mendelsohn, the musician; he would arrive on the astral plane and it would be like a policeman there to take away the Silver Cord and the Golden Bowl, and send him along to Patra. On Patra he would meet friends and acquaintances, and they would be able to discuss their past lives and carry out experiments which they had long wanted to do."

"Well, Master, what do they do about food here? There doesn't seem to be food, boxes of food, on this place which I assume is a dock."

"No, you won't find much food on this world. People don't need it. They pick up all their bodily and mental energy by a system of osmosis, that is, they absorb the energy given out by the light of Patra. If they want to eat for pleasure, of course, or drink for pleasure, then they are quite able to do so, except they cannot gormandise, and they cannot have those spiritous liquors which rot a person's brain. Such drinks are very, very bad, you know, and they can hold up a person's development for several lives.

"Now let's take a fleeting glance through the place. There is no time here, so it is useless for you to ask a person how long he has lived here because he will just look at you blankly and think you are someone not at all aware of the conditions. People never get used to Patra, they never get tired of it, there is always something fresh to do, fresh people to meet, but you cannot meet an enemy.

"Let us get up in the air and look down on this little fishing village."

"But I thought you said people did not need to eat, Master, so why should they want a fishing village?"

"Well, they are not catching fish in the ordinary meaning of the word, they are catching fish to see how they can be improved to give them better senses. On Earth, you know, the fish are really stupid and they deserve to get caught, but here they are caught in nets and kept in water all the time we have them, and they are treated kindly and there is no resentment from them. They realise that we are trying to do good for the whole species. Similarly with animals, none of them are afraid of mankind on this world. They are friends instead. But let's just take a darting visit to various places because soon we must be leaving here and going back to the Potala."

Suddenly I felt myself rising up into the air, and my sight seemed to be going. I suddenly got a splitting headache and, to tell the honest truth about it, I thought I was dying. The Lama Mingyar Dondup grabbed me and put his hands over my eyes. He said, "I am so sorry, Lobsang, I forgot you had not been treated for fourth dimension sight. We shall have to go down on the surface again for about half an hour." With that I felt myself sinking, and then the welcome, welcome feeling of something solid below my feet.

"This is the fourth dimension world, and sometimes there are overtones of the fifth dimension. If we are showing a person Patra then, of course, they have to have fourth dimensional vision otherwise it is too much of a strain for them." The Lama had me lay back on a couch and then he dropped things in my eyes. After several minutes he put goggles on me, goggles which completely covered my eyes. I said, "Oh! I can see now. This is wonderful." Before things had been beautiful, extraordinarily beautiful, but now that I could see in the fourth dimension the sights were so glorious that they just cannot be described in three dimensional words. But I nearly wore my eyes out looking about, and then we rose up into the air again and I just had not seen such beauty before. The men were of surpassing handsomeness, but the women—well, they were so beautiful that I felt somewhat strange stirrings inside, and, of course, women and I were strangers because my mother had been a very strict mother indeed, and my sister—well, I had hardly seen her. We were kept rigidly apart because it had been ordained before my birth that I should enter the Lamasery. But the beauty, the absolute beauty, and the tranquility, it really defies description in a three dimensional language. It is like trying to describe something on Earth by a man born blind. How is he going to describe colours? He is born blind, so what does he know about colours, what is there to describe? He can say something about the shape and about the weight, but the real beauty of the thing is absolutely beyond his comprehension. I am like that now, I have been treated to be able to see in the third dimension, the fourth dimension, and the fifth, so that when the time comes for me to leave this Earth I will go straight to Patra. So these people who say they have a course of instruction and it is run by Dr. Rampa by Ouija Board—well, they are just crackpots. I tell you again, when I leave this world I shall be completely beyond your reach. I shall be so far away from you that you cannot even comprehend it!

It is quite impossible for me to describe Patra to you. It is like trying to tell a person who is born blind what a picture exhibition is like—you would get nowhere.

But there are other things than pictures. Certain of the great people of old were here in this world of Patra and they were working to try to help other worlds, two dimensional worlds, and three dimensional worlds. Many of the so-called inventions on Earth are not inventions of the claimant; he or she just picked up the idea from something that he or she saw in the astral world, and he came back to Earth with a memory of something that had to be invented, he got the broad ideas of how to do it, and—well—he constructed whatever it was that had to be constructed and then he got it patented in his own name.

The Lama Mingyar Dondup seemed to be extraordinarily well known on Patra. He could go anywhere and meet anyone, and he introduced me as an old friend that the others remembered but I had forgotten because of the cloying clay of the Earth. They laughed with me, and said, "Never mind, you will soon be coming over to us and then you will remember everything."

The Lama Mingyar Dondup was talking to a scientist, and he was saying, "Of course the big trouble we have now is that people of different races have different outlooks. For instance, on some worlds women are treated as the equal of men, but on other worlds women are treated as common utensils or slaves, and when they get to a country which gives full freedom to women they are unnerved and absolutely lost. We

139

are working to try to find a way whereby all men and women of all countries will have a common viewpoint. They get a little way toward that in the astral world, but, of course, no one can come to Patra unless he realises to the full the rights of everyone." He looked at me and smiled, and then said, "I see you already recognise the rights of Friend Cat."

I replied, "Yes, sir, I love them. I think they are the most wonderful animals anywhere."

"You've got a marvellous reputation with animals, you know, and when you come back to us on Patra a whole horde of cats are going to be there to meet you. You will have a living fur coat." He smiled because this big brown and white cat was climbing up my front to sit on my shoulder, and, resting his left paw on my head so as to steady himself—just as a human would. The Lama Mingyar Dondup said, "Well, Bob, we've got to say goodbye to you for the time being, but Lobsang will soon be returning Home and then you will have ample opportunity to sit on his shoulder." Bob, the cat, nodded solemnly and jumped off onto a table, and he rubbed against me and purred and purred and purred.

The Lama Mingyar Dondup said, "Let's move to the other side of Patra. There is the kingdom of flowers and plants, and the trees especially are waiting to see you again." No sooner had he finished speaking than we arrived at this wonderful spot where there were incredibly beautiful flowers and trees. I was scared stiff to move for fear of treading on the flowers. The Lama looked at me and fully understood my predicament. He said, "Oh, I am so sorry, Lobsang, I should have told you. Here in the kingdom of flowers you have to lift yourself about a foot above the actual ground. It is one of the abilities of the fourth dimension. You think the ground is a foot higher, and so as you walk thinking the ground is a foot higher then you actually walk a foot above the soil in which these plants live. We won't risk anything now. Instead we will just take a look around some other parts of this world. The machine men, for instance." Machines with souls, flowers with souls, cats with souls. "I suppose we'd better be getting back, Lobsang," he said then, "because I have to show you a few things to prepare you in part for the life you are going to have to live. I wish I could travel with you and help you more, but my Kharma is that I am going to be killed by Communists who are going to stab me through the back. But, never mind that, let's go back to our own world."

CHAPTER NINE

We left what was called the "Four Dimension Room," and crossed the huge hall to the one which was marked "This World." The walk was about a quarter of a mile, so our feet were quite aching by the time we got to "This World."

The Lama Mingyar Dondup entered and sat on the bench next to the console. I followed him and sat down on the bench beside him. The Lama touched a button and the light in the room disappeared. Instead we could see our world in the dim, dim lighting. I looked away wondering what had happened, where was the light? And then I looked at the globe of the world—and promptly fell backwards over the bench, hitting my head on the hard floor. As I had looked into the world I saw a hideous dinosaur with jaws agape, and it was looking straight at me from a distance of about six feet.

I rather sheepishly picked myself up, ashamed that I had been frightened by a creature which had been dead thousands of years.

The Lama said, "We have to skim through some of the history because there is so much in the history books which is absolutely incorrect. Look!" On the world I saw a range of mountains, and at the foot of one of the mountains there was a great horde of soldiers and their camp followers which included many women. In those days, it seems, the soldiery could not do without the consolation of womens' bodies, so the women went to war with them so they could satisfy the men

142

after a victory. And if there was no victory the women were captured by the enemy and used for precisely the same purpose as they would have been used if their side had been victorious.

There was a very busy scene. Men were milling around quite a collection of elephants, and one man was standing on the broad back of an elephant arguing with the crowd below. "I tell you, these elephants will not cross the mountains where there is snow. They are used to heat, they cannot survive in the cold weather. In addition, how are we going to get the tons and tons of food which these elephants would need? I suggest that we unload the elephants and put the loads on horses native to the area. That is the only way we shall get across."

Well, the commotion went on, they were like a lot of old fishwives, arguing and waving their arms, but the elephant-man had his way, the elephants were unloaded and all the horses in the district were rounded up in spite of the protests of the farmers to whom they belonged.

Of course I did not understand a word of the speech, but this particular instrument which the Lama had just put on my head put all the knowledge of what was being said into my head instead of going by way of my ears. So I was able to follow everything in the most minute detail.

At last the immense cavalcade was ready, and the women were also put on horses. It is not generally realised that women are really much stronger physically than men. I supposed that they pretended to be weak because in that way men carried the loads and the women rode on ponies.

The cavalcade started off, up the mountain path, and as we progressed upwards we could see that there would have been no hope at all of getting the elephants up the narrow rocky path, and when we did encounter snow the horses did not think much of it, either, and they really had to be driven.

The Lama Mingyar Dondup skipped a few centuries,

143

and then when he stopped the spinning we saw there was a battle going on. We did not know where it was, but they seemed to be pretty bloody. It was not enough to stick a sword into a person, the victor used to cut off the head of the victim and the heads were all tossed in a great pile. We watched for a bit to see all these men killing each other, and there were flying pennants and hoarse cries, and at the sides of the battlefield the women watched from roughly made tents. It did not matter much to them which side won because they would be used for the same purpose. But they watched, I suppose, out of more or less idle curiosity the same as we were watching.

A touch of the knob, and the world spun faster. The Lama stopped it every so often, and it seemed utterly incredible to me that each time he stopped there seemed to be a war in progress. We moved on until we came to the time of the Crusaders, which the Lama had told me about. It was "the thing" in those days for men of title to go abroad and make war against the Saracens. The Saracens were a gentle, cultured race, but they were still quite prepared to defend their homeland, and many an English title ended on the battlefield.

At last we saw the Boer War in progress. Both sides were utterly convinced of the justice of their case, and the Boers seemed to have a particular target, not the heart, not the stomach, but lower so that if a man was wounded and if he was able to get home somehow, he would certainly be of no use to his wife. All this was explained to me in a whisper.

Then, all of a sudden, the battle ended. It seemed that both sides were either the winners or the losers because they intermingled and then, at last, the invaders—the Crusaders—moved to one side of the battlefield while the Saracens moved to the opposite side where they, too, had women waiting for them.

The wounded and the dying were left where they had fallen, there was nothing else that could be done. There was no medical service, so if a man was badly wounded he often asked his friends to put him out of his misery, and how they did that was to put a dagger in the man's hand and then move away. If the man really wanted to end his life he merely had to push the dagger into his heart.

The world spun on, and then there came a ferocious war which seemed to engulf most of the world. There were people of all colours fighting and using weapons, great guns on wheels, and in the air at the end of ropes there were things which I now know were called balloons. They were up high so that a man in a basket attached to the balloon could peer over the enemies' lines and try to figure out how they would attack or how they should be attacked. Then we saw some noisy machines come flying through the air, and they shot at the balloons and brought them down in flames.

The ground was an absolute morass of mud and blood, there were bits of humans all over the place. There were dead bodies suspended from barbed wire, and every so often there came a crump, crump, and great lumps would come flying through the air which, when they hit the ground, exploded with quite disastrous results to the countryside as well as to the enemy.

A touch of a button and the picture shifted. We were looking at the sea, and we could see dots so far away that they indeed looked like dots, but the Lama Mingyar Dondup brought them into closer focus and then we saw that they were huge metal vessels with long metal tubes which moved to and fro, and spewed out great missiles. The missiles travelled twenty miles or more before falling on an enemy ship. We saw one battleship, it must have been hit in the armament section, because we saw the missile land on the deck and then it was as if the world exploded, the vessel heaved and burst into thousands of parts. There were flying bits of metal all over the place, and flying bits of humans, and with all that blood coming down it seemed as if a red fog was settling over the place.

At last some sort of arrangement seemed to come into force because the soldiers stopped shooting at each other. We, from our vantage point, saw one man surreptitiously raise his weapon and shoot his commanding officer!

The Lama Mingyar Dondup quickly pressed a few buttons and we were back in the area of the Trojan Wars. I whispered, "Master, aren't we jumping from date to date without any regard for the sequence?"

"Oh, but I am showing you all this for a special reason, Lobsang. Look," he pointed. A Trojan soldier suddenly brought his spear to the level and it went straight through the heart of his commanding officer. "I was just showing you that human nature doesn't change. It goes on and on like this. You get a man, he will shoot his commanding officer, and then perhaps in another reincarnation he comes and does precisely the same thing again. I am trying to teach you certain things, Lobsang, not to teach you history as from a book because those history books are far too often altered to suit the political leaders of the time."

We sat there on our bench, and the Lama tuned us in to many different scenes. Sometimes there would be six hundred years between scenes. That certainly gave one an opportunity to judge what the politicos were really doing. We saw empires rise by arrant treachery, and we saw empires fall, again by arrant treachery.

The Lama suddenly said, "Now, Lobsang, here we will have a glimpse into the future." The globe darkened, lightened, and darkened again, and we saw strange sights. We saw a great liner as big as a city. It was steaming along like a queen of the seas, and all of a sudden there was a heart-breaking screech as the ship was sliced open below the waterline by a projection from a mighty iceberg.

The ship started to settle. There was a certain amount of panic, a lot of people got in lifeboats, others fell into the sea as the ship listed, and on one deck the band played to avert panic, the band played on until the ship went down with a frightening gurgle. Great bubbles of air came up, and great gouts of oil. Then gradually odd items came up as well, the dead body of a child, a woman's handbag which somehow floated to the surface. "This, Lobsang, is another item which is out of its chronological order. This should have come before the war you have just recently seen. But, never mind, you can flip through a picture book and perhaps get as much knowledge as if you read everything in that book in the right order. I am trying to get certain things into your head."

The dawn broke. The early morning sunlight glinted redly on the tips of the icebergs, and spread downwards as the sun rose higher. As it spread downwards it lost its red colour and became the ordinary, normal light of day.

The sea was littered with an absolutely incredible collection of items. Broken chairs and various parcels, and, of course, inevitably the dead bodies, white and waxy. There were men, or what had been men, in evening dress. There were women, or what had been women, also in evening dress, but which could better be described as evening undress.

We looked and we looked, and there were no rescue ships in sight, and as the Lama said, "Well, Lobsang, we will move on to something else, there is no point in us loitering here when there is not a thing that we can do." He put out his hand to the buttons and to the knob which was on the end of a little rod, and the globe spun faster. Daylight—darkness—darkness—daylight, and so on, and then we stopped. We were in a place called England, and my Guide translated some of the names for me. Piccadilly, Statue of Eros, and all sorts of things like that, and then he stopped right in front of a newspaper seller—of course we were quite invisible to the man because we were in a different time zone. What we were seeing now was what was yet to happen, we were glimpsing into the future. We were at the beginning of a century, but we were seeing something either 1939 or 1940, I could not quite make out the figures, not that it matters. But there were great placards about. The Lama read them out to me. They were about someone called Neville Chamberlain going

147

to Berlin with his umbrella. And then we slipped into what the Lama called a news theatre. On a screen we saw grim faced men in steel helmets and accoutered with all the instruments of war. They were marching in a most peculiar way, "The Goose Step," said the Lama, "practised a lot by the German army." And then the picture changed to show starving people in another part of the world, people who just dropped dead of hunger and cold.

We moved out into the street, and skipped a few days. And then the Lama stopped the spinning for us to catch our breath, etc., because skimming around the world through various eras of time was indeed quite a disturbing and exhausting experience, especially for me, a boy who had never been out of his own country, who had never seen things with wheels before. Yes, it was quite a disturbing thing.

I turned to the Lama Mingyar Dondup, and said, "Master, this matter of Patra; I have never heard of the place before, I have never heard any of the teachers mention Patra. They teach us that when we leave this Earth through the period of transition we go to the astral world, and there we live until the urge comes to us to go back to Earth in a different body or go to some other world in a different body. But nobody has said anything about Patra, and I am really confused."

"My dear Lobsang, there are many things of which you have not yet heard, but will. Patra is a world. It is a far superior world to this one and to the astral world. It is a world to which people go when they have some very special virtues, or when they have done a very great deal of good for others. It is not mentioned because it would be too discouraging. Many are chosen as possible material for Patra and then at the last moment the person shows some weakness or some wrongness of thought and so he loses his chance of going to Patra.

"You and I, Lobsang, are quite definitely assured of going to Patra as soon as we leave this world, but that is not the end of it because we shall live in Patra for a time and then we shall go to an even higher place. On Patra you see people who have devoted their time to research for the good of Man and Animals, not for Man alone, mind, but for the animal world as well. Animals have souls, and they progress or fail to progress just the same as humans do. Humans too often think that they are the Lords of Creation, and that an animal is just there for the use of Man. They could not be more mistaken!"

"Well, Master, you were showing me what war was like, a war that had lasted for years. Now I would like to see what happened, how it ended, etc."

"All right, then," said the Lama, "we will go to the time just before the ending of the war." He turned away from me and looked up some book with dates in it, and then he set the controls on the console and the simulacrum of our world came to life again, came to life with plenty of light.

We saw a shattered countryside, and with rails upon which they ran certain machines which carried goods or passengers. On this particular occasion there were what appeared to be some very ornate boxes on wheels. There were glass sides, and armed guards in great numbers patrolled all around. Then we saw servants putting out white cloths and covering tables, and dust covers were taken off various articles of furniture.

Then there came a lull. I took the opportunity to pay a visit to see that my own "nature" was in working order, and when I returned—oh, a couple of minutes later—I saw what seemed to be a vast number of people, I thought they were in fancy dress, but then I realised that these were head soldiers and head sailors. It seemed to be representatives from all the countries at war. One set of people did not associate with the other set of people. At last they were all arranged, and sitting at tables in that box-like thing which was some sort of vehicle.

I looked at them, and, of course, I had never seen anything like this before because all the leading men had medals, rows of them. Some had ribbons around their necks, also with medals attached, and I immediately recognised that these were the high members of a government trying to impress the other side by the weight of metal on their chests and the number of ribbons around their necks. It really astonished me how they could hear each other speak because of the jingle-jangle of this metal-wear on their chests. There was much waving of hands, and messengers were kept busy taking notes from one man to another, or even to another part of the vehicles. Of course, I had never seen a train before, and such a lot of it meant little to me at the time. Eventually they produced a document and it was passed from person to person, each who signed his name, and it really was most amazing the different types of signature, the different types of writing, and it appeared perfectly obvious to me that in all truth one side was no better than the other!

"That, Lobsang, has yet to come. This terrible war had been going on for several years, and they have now proposed and declared an armistice under which each side returns to their own country and tries to build up their shattered economy."

I looked, and I stared because there was no rejoicing here, everyone was grim-faced, and the looks were not of joy that the battle had ended, the looks were of hatred, deadly hatred which I could see from one side the thoughts were, "All right, you win this round, we'll get you next time."

The Lama Mingyar Dondup kept on to the same time. We saw soldiers and sailors and airmen still fighting until a certain hour of a certain day came round. They were still at war until that day and eleven o'clock appeared with, of course, the loss of countless lives. We saw a peaceful plane with red, white, and blue circles on it flying back to its base. It was five minutes past eleven, and then from the clouds there appeared a fighter plane, an evil looking thing it was, too. It roared down out of the clouds and got right behind the red, white, and blue plane, and then the pilot pressed a button in front of him and a stream of something came out of weapons and set the red, white, and blue plane on fire. It nosed downwards in flames, and then there was one final splash and bang, and that murder was committed. It was murder because the war had ended.

We saw great vessels upon the seas loaded with troops returning to their own countries. They were absolutely loaded, so many that some of the men had to sleep on deck, some had to sleep in the lifeboats, but the ships were all going toward a very large country whose policies I could not understand because in the first case they were selling weapons to both sides, and then, when eventually they joined in the war—well, they were fighting against their own weapons. I thought that this surely must be the depths of insanity.

As the great ships reached the harbour the whole place seemed to go wild with excitement. Skeins of paper were flung about as streamers, cars were hooting, the ships were hooting as well, and everywhere there were bands playing, no matter that some were playing one piece of music and another lot was playing another piece of music. The uproar was indescribable.

Later we saw what appeared to be one of the leaders of the victorious forces driving down a vast street with huge buildings on each side, and from all the floors of the buildings there came pelting paper confetti, paper ribbons, and all that type of thing. Various people were blowing hard on some sort of instrument which certainly could not be called a musical instrument. It seemed that there was a great celebration because now much profit would be made from the sale of ex-Government weapons to other countries, smaller countries, who wanted to have a go at war with some neighbour.

It was a dismal scene indeed which appeard on this world. The soldiers, the sailors, and the airmen had returned to their homeland, victorious, they thought, but now—well, what were they going to do for a living? There were millions of people out of work. There was no money, and many of them had to queue up and go

151

to what they called a "soup kitchen" once a day. There they got some awful muck in a can which they then took home to share with their families.

The outlook was grim indeed. In one country ragged wretches could continue no longer, they were walking along on the sidewalks, peering at the space where the sidewalk became the pavement, the roadway, they were looking for a crust or anything, a cigarette butt, anything at all. And then they would stop and lean against perhaps one of the posts which carried wires, notices or lights, and then they would slump to the ground and roll into the gutter—dead, dead of starvation, dead through loss of hope. Instead of sorrow from onlookers there was gladness, some more people had died, surely soon there would be enough jobs. But no, these "soup kitchens" grew in number, and various uniformed people went about picking up the dead and putting them on a wagon to be taken away to be—I supposed—buried or burnt.

We watched various items spread out over the years, and then in one country we saw they were preparing for war again, the country which lost last time. There were great preparations, youth movements, and all the rest of it. They got flying training by making quite a number of small aircraft and claiming that these were recreational things.

We saw a very funny little man with a small moustache and pale, bulging eyes. Whenever he appeared and started ranting then a crowd quickly collected. Things like this were going on all over the world, and in many cases countries went to war. Eventually there was a very big war in which most of the world was involved.

"Master," I said, "I cannot understand how you can conjure up pictures of things which have not yet occurred."

The Lama looked at me and then he looked at the machine standing ready to show us more pictures. "Well, Lobsang, actually there is nothing very difficult in it, because if you get a gang of people you can just about bet all you have that when they do things they will all do it in the same way. If a woman is being pursued by a man she will run in one direction and hide. Now if that occurs a second and a third time her path is established, and you are very sure then when you predict that there will be a fourth occasion and the woman will run to her secret hiding place, and that her tormentor will soon be caught."

"But, sir," I said, "how is it possible to produce pictures of a thing that hasn't happened?"

"Unfortunately, Lobsang, you are not old enough yet to be able to appreciate an explanation, but briefly, corresponding things happen in the fourth dimension and we get what is more or less an echo down here on the third dimension. Some people have the ability to see far ahead, and to know exactly what is happening. I am one of those called a very sensitive clairvoyant and telepath, but you are going to surpass me many, many times because you have been trained like this almost before you were born. You have thought that your family have been hard on you. Yes, they have, very hard, but this was an order from the Gods. You have a special task to do, and you had to be taught anything which could be useful to you. When you are older you will understand about time tracks and different dimensions, and all that sort of thing. I told you yesterday about crossing an imaginary line on the Earth, and finding that you were in a different day. That, of course, is an entirely artificial affair so that the countries of the world can trade, and so they have this artificial system where time is artificially varied.

"Lobsang, there is a point which you apparently have not noticed. The things we are seeing now, and discussing now, are things that will not happen until fifty years or so have passed."

"I was almost stunned when you told me that, Master, because at the time it seemed all natural, but—yes—I can see now that some of the things—well, we don't have the science to do them. Therefore it must be something in the future."

The Lama nodded his head gravely and said, "Yes, in 1930 or 1940, or somewhere in-between there, the second World War will begin. And war will rage almost throughout the whole of the globe. It will bring absolute ruin to some countries, and the ones who win the war will lose the peace, and those who lose the war will win the peace. I cannot tell you when the war will actually start because there is no point in knowing, anyhow, we cannot do anything about it. But it should be round about 1939, and that is a good few years ahead yet."

"After that war—the second Great War—there will be continuous guerilla warfare, continuous strikes, and all the time the Unions will be trying to increase their power and gain control of their countries.

"I am sorry to tell you that in about 1985 some strange event will occur which will set the scene for the third Great World War. That war will be between peoples of all nationalities and all colours, and it will bring the Race of Tan into being. Rapes are terrible things, no doubt, but at least if a black man rapes a white woman then we have yet another colour—tan, the Race of Tan. We have to have a uniform colour on this Earth. That is one of the very necessary things before there can be much lasting peace.

"We cannot give exact dates, exact to the day, the hour, the minute and the second as some idiots think we can, but we can say that round about the year 2000 there will be intense activity in the Universe, and intense activity on this world. After a bitter, bitter struggle the war will be resolved with help from people from outer space, people who do not like Communism here.

"But now is the time to see if my legs are good enough to walk on and get down the mountainside, because then we must return to the Potala."

We looked at all the machines we had used, we made sure they were clean and left in the best condition that we could manage. We made sure that all the switches were working properly, and then the Lama Mingyar

Dondup and I put on new robes, "new" robes, a million or more years old and of wonderful material. We must have looked like two old washerwomen if anybody could have seen us poring over the clothes to find something which especially appealed to that amount of vanity which we still had within us. At last we were satisfied. I was a monk, and Mingyar Dondup was done up with a robe of very high status indeed, and I knew he was entitled to an even higher one.

We found big robes which would fit over our new equipment, and so we put them on to save our clothes when going down the mountainside.

We had a meal and a drink, and we each said goodbye to that little room with the hole in the corner. Then we set out.

"Master!" I exclaimed, "How are we going to hide the entrance?"

"Lobsang, never doubt the Powers that Be. It is already arranged that when we leave this place a curtain of solid stone, many feet thick, will slip down and cover the entrance, and destroy any evidence of it from outside. So when we get out we must hold our hands and rush, we must go as fast as we can together to get out before the big rock falls in place and seals away these secrets to prevent the Chinese finding them, because, as I told you, the Chinese will take over this country and Tibet will be no more. Instead there will be a secret Tibet with the wisest of Wise Men living in caves and tunnels like this, and these men will teach the men and women of a new generation which will follow much later on, and which will bring peace to this Earth."

We traversed the path, and then we saw a square of daylight. We hurried along as fast as we could, and shot out into the open air. I looked with love down at the Potala, and down at Chakpori, and then I looked at the steep way ahead of us and I really wondered how we would manage.

At that moment there was a tremendous commotion, as if the world was coming to an end. The rock door had fallen, and we could hardly believe our eyes. There was no trace of an opening, no trace of a path. It was as though this adventure had never been.

So we made our way down the mountainside, and I looked at my Guide, and I thought of him going to die at the treacherous hands of Communists. And I thought of my own death which would occur in a foreign country. But then the Lama Mingyar Dondup and I would be united in Sacred Patra.

*　*　*

EPILOGUE

And so yet another true story has come to an end. Now there is nothing except to wait in my hospital bed until my Silver Cord be severed and my Golden Bowl be shattered, so that I can go to my Spiritual Home— Patra.

There is so much I could have done. I would have liked, for instance, to have spoken in the League of Nations, or whatever they call themselves nowadays, on behalf of Tibet. But there was too much jealousy, too much spite, and the Dalai Lama was in a difficult position taking aid from people, so that, of course, he could not go against their wishes.

I could have written more about Tibet, but here again there was jealousy and fake articles, and the press have always sought for anything gruesomely horrifying or what they call "wicked" and which they do every day.

Transmigration is true. It is an actual fact of life, and it used to be a great science indeed. It is like a man travelling by air to his destination and then finding a car waiting for him as he steps out of the plane, only in this a Great Spirit takes over a body that he may do a task allotted to him.

These books, my books, are true, absolutely true, and if you think that this particular book smacks of science fiction you are wrong. The science in it could have been many times increased had the scientists been at all interested, but the fiction—there just isn't any, not even "artists' license."

157

So I lay back in my old hospital bed waiting release from the long night of horror which is "life" on Earth. My cats have been a relief and a joy, and I love them more than I love a human.

Just a final word. Some people have tried to "cash in" on me already. Some people spread about the story that I was dead, and that from the "Other Side" I had commanded them to start a correspondence course, that I (from the "Other Side") would be the head of it and we would correspond with the Ouija Board. Now, the Ouija Board is absolute fakery, and worse, because in some cases it can allow evil or mischievous entities to take possession of the person using the Ouija Board.

May the Good Spirits preserve you.

THE END

THREE LIVES
by T. Lobsang Rampa

This book continues the theme of Dr Rampa's previous book
I BELIEVE in that it is a further statement of his personal
belief in life after death, and his thoughts on the nature of the
afterlife. Free from prejudice, free from the dogmas of orga-
nized religion, Dr Rampa's beliefs have been formed by years
of study, years of offering comfort and inspiration to his countless followers all over the world.

THREE LIVES will be welcomed by the many thousands of
readers who turn to Dr Rampa for consolation and guidance.

0   552   10707   7   75p

AS IT WAS!
by T. Lobsang Rampa

The Chief Astrologer of Tibet had been summoned to proclaim
the horoscope of the six-year-old Lobsang, son of Lord and
Lady Rampa. It was the most difficult reading, the hardest life
he had ever encountered, the old man said. The boy was going
to learn all the medical arts of Tibet, and then journey to China
to study medicine in the Western style. He would know immense suffering and dreadful hardship, travel in many countries, be unjustly imprisoned. But above all, the boy's lonely
destiny would be to carry out a great task of the utmost importance to all humanity—and evil forces would work against
him to thwart his efforts . . .

AS IT WAS! is a fascinating account of the life and achieve-
ments of a remarkable man.

0   552   10087   0   £1.00

A SELECTED LIST OF PSYCHIC, MYSTIC AND OCCULT TITLES FROM CORGI

☐	09828 0	The Prophecies of Nostradamus	*Erika Cheetham*	£1.50
☐	08800 5	Chariot of the Gods?	*Erich Von Daniken*	95p
☐	09083 2	Return to the Stars	*Erich Von Daniken*	95p
☐	09689 X	The Gold of the Gods	*Erich Von Daniken*	£1.25
☐	10073 0	In Search of Ancient Gods	*Erich Von Daniken*	85p
☐	10371 3	Miracles of the Gods	*Erich Von Daniken*	85p
☐	10870 7	According to the Evidence	*Erich Von Daniken*	£1.25
☐	11020 5	The Ghost of Flight 401	*John G. Fuller*	£1.25
☐	11220 8	My Search for the Ghost of Flight 401	*Elizabeth Fuller*	£1.00
☐	09430 7	The U.F.O. Experience—A Scientific Inquiry	*J. Allen Hynek*	95p
☐	10928 2	The Ancient Magic of the Pyramids	*Ken Johnson*	80p
☐	13374 8	Life After Life	*Raymond A. Moody Jr. M.D.*	95p
☐	11140 X	Reflections on Life After Life	*Raymond A. Moody Jr. M.D.*	95p
☐	10707 7	Three Lives	*T. Lobsang Rampa*	75p
☐	10628 3	Doctor From Lhasa	*T. Lobsang Rampa*	85p
☐	11464 2	The Cave of the Ancients	*T. Lobsang Rampa*	£1.00
☐	10416 7	I Believe	*T. Lobsang Rampa*	75p
☐	10189 3	The Saffron Robe	*T. Lobsang Rampa*	85p
☐	10087 0	As It Was!	*T. Lobsang Rampa*	£1.00
☐	09834 5	The Third Eye	*T. Lobsang Rampa*	£1.00
☐	11413 8	The Rampa Story	*T. Lobsang Rampa*	95p
☐	11283 6	Autumn Lady	*Mama San Ra-Ab Rampa*	85p
☐	11315 8	Ghosts of Wales	*Peter Underwood*	£1.25

CORGI BOOKS, Cash Sales Department, P.O. Box 11, Falmouth, Cornwall.

Please send cheque or postal order, no currency.

U.K. Please allow 30p for the first book, 15p for the second book and 12p for each additional book ordered to a maximum charge of £1.29.

B.F.P.O. and **Eire** allow 30p for the first book, 15p for the second book plus 12p per copy for the next 7 books, thereafter 6p per book.

Overseas Customers. Please allow 50p for the first book and 15p per copy for each additional book.

NAME (Block Letters) ....

ADDRESS ....

....